National Trust
SIMPLY BAKING

National Trust

SIMPLY BAKING

Sybil Kapoor

National Trust

For Raju, with love

First published in the United Kingdom in 2012 by
National Trust Books
10 Southcombe Street
London W14 0RA

An imprint of Anova Books Ltd

Text and recipes © Sybil Kapoor, 2012
Copyright © National Trust Books, 2012

The moral rights of the author have been asserted.

ISBN: 9781907892325

A CIP catalogue record for this book is available from the British Library.

20 19 18 17 16 15 14 13 12
10 9 8 7 6 5 4 3 2 1

Reproduction by Mission Productions Ltd, Hong Kong
Printed in Malaysia by Vivar Printing Sdn. Bhd.

Senior Commissioning Editor: Cathy Gosling
Senior Editor: Kristy Richardson
Copy Editor: Maggie Ramsay
Designer: Nicola Collings
Proofreader: Alyson Silverwood
Photography: Karen Thomas
Photography Assistant: Laura Urschel
Food Styling: Bridget Sargeson, Jack Sargeson
Prop Styling: Cynthia Inions

This book can be ordered direct from the publisher at the website:
www.anovabooks.com, or try your local bookshop. Also available at
National Trust shops or www.shop.nationaltrust.org.uk.

CONTENTS

NOTES

Temperatures given are for a fan oven. This method of heat is now widely used for electric ovens. It ensures that the oven temperature is the same at the top of the oven as at the bottom. If you have a conventional oven, increase the temperature by about 10°C and cook in the centre of the oven unless otherwise specified. Ovens can vary greatly in temperature, and there is difference of 10–20°C between fan and conventional ovens. Many recipe books allow a 20°C difference, but I find this too large. It is important to follow your instinct when baking and to check dishes shortly before they're due to be ready. I have adjusted the gas marks so that they work for each recipe; they are not necessarily the exact equivalent because gas ovens are not fan-assisted.

Where possible, I use British ingredients.

Butter is unsalted. This allows you to control the taste of each recipe more accurately.

For greasing cake tins, it's better to use oil rather than butter as this prevents an uneven colouring of the sides of a cake. If you would like to use British-grown oil, buy a cold-pressed rapeseed oil.

Choose British organic or Freedom Food free-range eggs, medium-sized unless specified.

Salt is fine British sea salt, unless specified.

I like the pure taste of refined caster sugar and use it in most recipes. You can use unrefined caster sugar: it gives a more complex, caramelised flavour.

I use organic lemons, but you can use any other unwaxed lemons. Always wash and pat dry lemons before using.

Pastry weight: traditional British recipes for pies and tarts give the weight of the flour (the main component of the pastry) to describe the pastry weight. This is not the same weight as a pack of ready-made pastry. See page 76 for more information about pastry.

If you love cooking from old British recipe books, it is helpful to know the following:
½ gill is 70ml/2½ fl oz
1 gill is 140ml/¼ pint
1 (British) quart is 2 pints or ¼ gallon/1.140 litres

(GF) **indicates that the recipe is gluten-free**

Weights

7.5g	¼ oz
15g	½ oz
20g	¾ oz
30g	1oz
35g	1¼ oz
40g	1½ oz
50g	1¾ oz
55g	2oz
60g	2¼ oz
70g	2½ oz
80g	2¾ oz
85g	3oz
90g	3¼ oz
100g	3½ oz
115g	4oz
125g	4½ oz
140g	5oz
150g	5½ oz
170g	6oz
185g	6½ oz
200g	7oz
225g	8oz
250g	9oz
285g	10oz
300g	10½ oz
310g	11oz
340g	12oz
370g	13oz
400g	14oz
425g	15oz
450g	1lb
500g	1lb 2oz
565g	1¼ lb
680g	1½ lb
700g	1lb 9oz
750g	1lb 10oz
800g	1¾ lb
900g	2lb
1kg	2lb 3oz
1.1kg	2lb 7oz
1.4kg	3lb
1.5kg	3½ lb
1.8kg	4lb
2kg	4½ lb
2.3kg	5lb
2.7kg	6lb
3.1kg	7lb
3.6kg	8lb
4.5kg	10lb

Oven temperatures

	Fan	Conventional	Gas
Very cool	100°C	110°C/225°F	Gas ¼
Very cool	120°C	130°C/250°F	Gas ½
Cool	130°C	140°C/275°F	Gas 1
Slow	140°C	150°C/300°F	Gas 2
Moderately slow	160°C	170°C/325°F	Gas 3
Moderate	170°C	180°C/350°F	Gas 4
Moderately hot	180°C	190°C/375°F	Gas 5
Hot	190°C	200°C/400°F	Gas 6
Very hot	200°C	220°C/425°F	Gas 7
Very hot	220°C	230°C/450°F	Gas 8
Hottest	230°C	240°C/475°F	Gas 9

Volume

5ml	1 teaspoon	
10ml	1 dessertspoon	
15ml	1 tablespoon	
30ml	1fl oz	
40ml	1½ fl oz	
55ml	2fl oz	
70ml	2½ fl oz	
85ml	3fl oz	
100ml	3½ fl oz	
120ml	4fl oz	
130ml	4½ fl oz	
150ml	5fl oz	
170ml	6fl oz	
185ml	6½ fl oz	
200ml	7fl oz	
225ml	8fl oz	
250ml	9fl oz	
270ml	9½ fl oz	
285ml	10fl oz	½ pint
300ml	10½ fl oz	
345ml	12fl oz	
400ml	14fl oz	
425ml	15fl oz	¾ pint
450ml	16fl oz	
465ml	16½ fl oz	
565ml	20fl oz	1 pint
700ml	25fl oz	1¼ pints
750ml	26fl oz	
850ml	30fl oz	1½ pints
1 litre	35fl oz	1¾ pints
1.5 litres	53fl oz	2½ pints

Length

3mm	⅛ in
5mm	¼ in
1cm	½ in
2cm	¾ in
2.5cm	1in
6cm	2½ in
7cm	2¾ in
7.5cm	3in
9cm	3½ in
10cm	4in
18cm	7in
20cm	8in
22cm	8½ in
23cm	9in
25cm	10in
27cm	11in
30cm	12in
35cm	14in
38cm	15in

INTRODUCTION

THE KITCHEN

There are few things as enjoyable as spending time in the kitchen making a cake or a few scones. The simple act of baking engenders a sense of happiness. The perfect excuse, if one were needed, for sharing such pleasures in this book.

Over the years, many excellent baking books have been written, some of which offer technical advice alongside their recipes, but none, as far as I know, have looked at baking from the perspective of our food and landscape.

As you turn these pages, you will find yourself in different places: first the kitchen, then the dairy, followed by the mill. You will step out into a kitchen garden, linger in an age-old orchard and wander down the hedgerows looking for blackberries, before returning to your kitchen with its larder filled with sugar and spice.

Each of these resources has shaped British baking for hundreds of years. The bountiful supply of butter, cream and milk from the dairy has enabled us to create buttery cakes, fragile cheesecakes and baked cream puddings. The mill has provided us with soft wheat flours that are perfect for biscuits, cakes and pastries. Thanks to our orchards, we have developed an amazing range of baked fruit puddings and cakes, while exotic spices and dried fruit have enriched our repertoire of fruit cakes, breads and pastries since medieval times.

However, this is not a book about capturing the past – quite the opposite. This is a book about British baking both now and in the future. To be creative, you have to understand your materials and their context. As seasonality and local sourcing become increasingly important, British cooking will inevitably change. The question is, in what way?

Through the course of this book, and with the help of the National Trust, I've tried to look at our baking ingredients afresh by putting them into their cultural context. I've drawn inspiration from the Trust's amazing range of properties, from its working water mills such as Clyston Mill in Devon, to its pretty dairies, like that at Uppark House in West Sussex. With such examples, who wouldn't feel tempted to use fragrant local flour or see dairy produce in a new light? Town-based as I am, it's impossible not to daydream about changing how we all shop, cook and eat after wandering through one of the Trust's many restored orchards and kitchen gardens, like those on the Brockhampton Estate in Herefordshire and Knightshayes Court in Devon.

ABOVE LEFT Enamel kitchenware on a two-ring cooker in the kitchen at 59 Rodney Street, Liverpool.

ABOVE RIGHT The 'New Gold Medal Eagle' range, installed c.1895, in the kitchen at Uppark, West Sussex.

Over the last few years, the National Trust has been working towards connecting people more closely with the landscape and food production. Their remit has covered every conceivable aspect of food production from sustainable farming and community allotments to growing and rearing local and seasonal food for use in their own restaurants and to sell in their shops. Once you start to experience such schemes, it is hard not to be seduced by their potential. After all, it is you and I who ultimately dictate how our food is grown by how we shop.

The first two chapters – The Dairy and The Mill – deal with primary baking ingredients, such as butter, cream, eggs and flour. As a result, these chapters are filled with essential baking know-how. You cannot think of baking with eggs or butter without learning about the different ways to make cakes, or of using flour without instructions for making pastry and bread.

The emphasis changes slightly in the next four chapters by focusing on different sources of ingredients, such as the orchard or hedgerow. This enables the cook to follow the seasons and make full use of what is available. The Kitchen Garden, for example, is divided into the following sections: flowers & herbs, shoots, vegetables, soft fruit, and roots. Each section examines how best to use its featured ingredients in baking, whether it be flavouring meringues with lavender by folding lavender flowers into the whipped egg white or using grated carrots to create a moist carrot pudding with cardamom lemon syrup.

As the book is subdivided in this way, I've included cross-references, because some categories of recipes, such as muffins or soufflés, appear in different sections in the book. Those in search of inspiration should also glance through the index.

I hope you will find plenty of new ideas to expand your baking repertoire. I particularly love the elderflower and gooseberry curd cake, water biscuits, and plum and damson cobbler. Forgive the omission of some old favourites, but if you love gingerbread and flapjacks you should try the National Trust's delicious sticky ginger tray bake.

No kitchen is complete without at least one battered reference book that you can turn to when in need of help. Since I love such books, I've tried to include as much practical information as possible throughout the book.

On which note, it seems fitting to return to the kitchen, the starting point of this book. Over the years, I have cooked in many different kitchens, from the cool Victorian rectory kitchen of my childhood, with its huge painted dresser and north-facing windows, to my current urban basement kitchen, all German minimalism with clean lines and soft light. In between, I've experienced everything from gleaming stainless steel restaurant kitchens to bedsits with little more than a Baby Belling, kettle and sink.

No matter how small the kitchen, I step into another world when I bake – a sensation that I suspect is familiar to many cooks. Maybe it is the peculiar mix of precision and creativity that baking demands which takes you into another zone. As your hands are exercised by practical tasks such as beating or kneading, your mind drifts away on the currents of evocative smells. I can be in London on a hot summer's day, but if I whisk up the strawberry cream cake my mother used to make for my father's birthday, I find myself back in a rural English garden, transported by the sweet scent of sugared sponge and ripe strawberries.

We are the most recent links in a long line of cooks who, over the centuries, have created new and wonderful dishes. An Elizabethan cook at Canons Ashby in Northamptonshire would have delighted in the luxury of having a beehive oven set within the wall of the newly built kitchen, rather than in an outbuilding. They could now comfortably bake fantastic pies, all the rage, for their employers the Dryden family. In much the same way, we might greet the arrival of the latest hi-tech oven, allowing us to whisk up a dozen pretty fairy cakes in the blink of an eye.

British cooking is continually evolving in response to the ingredients we buy and the equipment we use. Who could resist stepping into the kitchen to bake some tempting new concoction? Not I.

RIGHT The stone-flagged kitchen at Canons Ashby, Northamptonshire.

A GUIDE TO BAKING

This section is for dipping into if you are a first-time baker or have one of those niggling baking questions.

UNDERSTANDING OVENS

Every oven is different. It's been my experience that ovens vary enormously in how they cook, and whenever I've moved home it's taken time to learn the idiosyncrasies of an unfamiliar oven. Don't be afraid to alter a cooking time or temperature if your recipe is cooking too fast or too slowly.

EQUIPMENT

The wonderful thing about baking is that you can start with very little equipment, provided you don't mind doing things by hand. As your interest grows, you can buy more utensils to suit your needs. For many years I didn't have a pastry brush or even a potato peeler, let alone a food processor or electric whisk. Each purchase was a luxury that added to my pleasure in baking.

The bare essentials

Weighing scale – vital to ensure perfect results.

Large metal spoon – allows you to 'fold' ingredients together, for example when mixing whipped egg whites into melted chocolate.

Two wooden spoons – essential in any kitchen.

Three or four round-bottomed mixing bowls, from large to small – you always need them.

Knives – every cook needs good knives, starting with a small stainless-steel serrated knife and a sharp stainless-steel chef's knife. These will enable you to prepare everything from fruit to chopped herbs. You also need a good stainless-steel bread knife for slicing cakes as well as bread.

Rolling pin – ideally, a long wooden one with no handles.

Stainless-steel sieve – always useful, robust and dishwasher-proof.

Balloon whisk – indispensable for whipping cream and whisking eggs.

Measuring jug – invaluable, especially if you have a non-drip version.

Rectangular wire rack – essential for cooling baked items.

Four-sided grater – perfect for everything from nutmeg to carrot.

Kitchen scissors – you will need these for cutting baking parchment to line cake tins.

Baking parchment or greaseproof paper – helps ensure food doesn't stick. If you use greaseproof, you must grease the tin and then the paper.

Tins and baking dishes

Buying baking tins and sheets is like buying shoes – they come in all sorts of tempting shapes and sizes, from dainty dariole moulds to big Christmas cake tins. As a golden rule, go for quality. You want sturdy, non-stick tins that conduct heat evenly and don't warp or rust. Black-lined tins are best at conducting heat.

Here's a beginner's list to get you started:

- Two or three flat baking sheets – preferably heavy and non-stick.
- Two 18cm/7in or 20cm/8in sandwich tins.
- One 20cm/8in spring-form tin – a deep-sided tin that unclips to remove the sides from the base. Useful for deep cakes and cheesecakes.
- One 18 x 28cm/7 x 11in tray bake tin.
- One Swiss roll tin, 20 x 30cm/8 x 12in.
- One 900g/2lb and one 450g/1lb loaf tin.
- One 12-hole muffin tray.
- One 12-hole bun tray – with smaller holes than a muffin tray; this is used for fairy cakes and English cupcakes and used to be called a patty tin tray.
- Eight 150ml/5fl oz pudding basins.
- Eight 150ml/5fl oz china ramekins.
- Assorted china pie and gratin dishes.

Desirables

Food mixers versus food processors – most cooks have one or the other but not both. I currently have a food processor, which I use for blending and mixing, but it means that I have to take care not to over-process mixtures, and I always have to finish delicate mixes such as cakes by hand in a bowl. Food processors don't beat air into mixtures as effectively as a food mixer and tend to overheat dough mixes. Food mixers, on the other hand, are excellent at whisking, beating and kneading dough, but they do take up a lot of space. Ultimately, your choice will depend on your needs overall as a cook.

Set of measuring spoons – it's amazing how ordinary spoons can vary in size, so for fail-safe cooking it really is worth buying a set of standard measuring spoons. I always use level spoonfuls in my recipes unless specified otherwise.

Pastry cutters – plain or fluted round metal cutters that usually come in a set of different sizes. Perfect for scones, biscuits, small tarts and canapés. If you love making biscuits, buy different shapes such as stars or hearts.

Spatula – a flexible plastic spatula is invaluable for scraping mixture out of mixing bowls and food processors.

Palette knife – this flexible, broad-bladed knife with a rounded end is useful for spreading fillings and icing and for lifting biscuits off baking sheets. Start with a large one and later add a small one to your collection.

Pastry brush – invaluable for glazing and greasing; try not to frizzle the ends by applying to hot surfaces.

Baking beans – these baking weights are used on top of a piece of baking paper when baking a pastry case without a filling (in other words, baking blind). You can buy ceramic or metal beans or use uncooked dried beans or rice. Store separately so you don't inadvertently use them in another recipe. Ceramic beans conduct heat more effectively and will cook your pastry more quickly than dried beans – but all will prevent the pastry from puffing up and cracking.

Nylon piping bag – aside from icing, they're useful for piping choux buns and éclairs. You can also buy disposable ones or make your own by placing one small polythene bag in another and snipping off one corner to form the nozzle.

Icing nozzles – these come in many sizes and can be plain or star-shaped, plastic or metal – just slip into your piping bag. The most useful sizes are 5mm/¼ in and 1cm/½ in.

Cake skewer – a long, flat-sided metal skewer is useful for testing whether a cake is cooked. Insert into the deepest part of the cake and pull out. If the skewer comes out clean, the cake is cooked. You can use a knife, but it will leave a slight gash in the surface of the cake.

BAKING KNOW-HOW

Successful baking depends on following a recipe accurately. If you're new to baking, you may find some of the terms used in recipes unfamiliar. They've developed over the centuries as a form of culinary shorthand to explain precisely what is needed. It's currently unfashionable to use many of these terms as some editors fear that it will discourage the reader from following the recipe. My view is that knowledge is power and that if you fully understand what terms such as 'scald' or 'fold' mean, you will feel empowered to cook a recipe correctly. Here are a few common terms:

Baking blind – for ultra-crispy pastry, line a chilled, raw pastry tart case with baking parchment, fill with baking beans, and bake until the pastry is partially or fully cooked. Remove the weighted paper for the last five minutes of cooking time.

To beat – this term often confuses people, including food writers! In baking recipes, it usually refers to using a wooden spoon or a food mixer to vigorously mix together several ingredients until they're well mixed. It does not refer to a fine whisk. However, you can use the thick whisk attachment of a hand-held mixer – which may partly explain the confusion. When it refers to eggs, it means using a fork to roughly mix the yolks with the whites, or simply to break down the egg white slightly.

To cream – to beat together butter and sugar with a wooden spoon, in a food processor or in a food mixer with a beater attachment until enough air has been incorporated into the mixture to make it pale and fluffy.

Dropping consistency – when a mixture will literally drop easily from a spoon if given a sharp shake.

To dust – to lightly coat a surface by sifting the stated ingredient through a fine sieve. For example, when preparing a cake tin, you would dust it with plain flour, or when finishing a cake you might dust it with icing sugar.

To fold – this is when you combine two mixtures, one of which is lightened with the addition of air, such as whipped egg whites or cream. You need a flattish metal spoon to cut down into the heavier of the two mixtures and scoop up the heavier mixture from the base of the bowl to layer it on top of the lighter mixture, until the two are evenly integrated while still retaining lots of air bubbles. Recipe books often tell you to work quickly, but according to food science writer Harold McGee in *McGee on Food and Cooking* (2004), it is much more effective to work slowly and gently. Having tested it out, I would agree – fold your mixtures in a slow, gentle, loving manner and you will have the fluffiest cakes and soufflés.

To grease – to lightly oil or butter a cake tin or baking sheet to prevent its future contents from sticking once they're baked. The easiest ways to do this are either to dip some kitchen paper in oil and rub over the baking tin or melt some butter and brush over the tin. Most bakers also grease non-stick containers and line them with baking parchment. There is nothing worse than seeing a beautiful cake or tart break as it sticks to its container.

To knead – see full instructions on how to knead bread dough on page 110. To knead pastry or scone dough, turn the roughly mixed dough out of its bowl on to a work surface and gently press the mixture and partially fold the dough under itself until it forms a smooth ball. Try not to handle it too much.

To pare – to remove thin strips of orange or lemon zest, using a potato peeler. Try to avoid taking off too much of the bitter white pith.

To scald – to heat a liquid to just below boiling point. In other words, when little bubbles form around the edge of the pan and it starts to steam. Don't let it bubble up into a full boil.

How to line a round cake tin – this is useful for slow-cooked or fragile cakes. Lightly oil the cake tin. Using the base of the tin as a template, cut three circles of baking parchment. Place one in the bottom of the tin. Measure the depth of the tin, add an extra 2.5cm/1in and cut a band of baking parchment long enough to fit around the inside of the tin. Make a 1cm/½ in deep fold lengthways down one long side and snip into this every 1cm/½ in or so, at a slight angle, so that once it is pressed around the cake tin's side, the snipped surface will lie flat on the bottom of the tin. Place a second paper disc over this and lightly oil the lined bottom and sides of the tin. It is now ready to be filled. The third disc of paper is for covering the top of the cake later in the cooking process to prevent it from scorching.

How to line a Swiss roll tin – cut a piece of baking parchment slightly larger than your tin. Lightly oil the tin. Fold each edge of the baking parchment so that it forms a 2.5cm/1in margin. Press the paper into the tin to fit neatly and line the sides.

THE
DAIRY

THE DAIRY

One of the first things anyone minded to bake does is open the fridge door to check whether they have enough butter or eggs to make their chosen dish. Dairy products are so integral to our cooking we barely consider them as ingredients in their own right. We take for granted the fact that we have a constant, rather than seasonal, supply of good-quality butter, milk and eggs. Yet such foods lie at the heart of our cooking. Appreciate their characteristics and you will hold the key to British baking.

Imagine for a moment that instead of peering into your fridge, you're stepping into the eighteenth-century dairy of a country house. Scrubbed clean and scented by the fresh sweet milk, its cool tiled shelves hold pots of freshly skimmed cream and churns of milk. More cream has been churned for butter, and the butter is being washed and beaten in fresh water to rid it of any acidic buttermilk, which would turn it rancid. Freshly shaped butter pats are chilling on the stone or tiled shelves. Some of the abundant rich golden summer butter has to be heavily salted to preserve it for the winter months. The paler winter-milk butter and whey butter might be dyed yellow with marigold petals or carrot juice to make it look as good as the creamier summer butter. Later, the remaining whole and semi-skimmed milk will be turned into cheese. Nothing is wasted. The whey is saved from the dripping cheese curds and used to make tangy whey butter or served as a refreshing drink. The buttermilk drained from the butter churn is used to make scones.

Were you the house's cook, you would instruct the dairymaid of what you needed sent to the kitchen, and would ensure that the poultry man supplied you with sufficient eggs. There are curds to make, custard tarts and creams to bake, and buttery cakes to serve.

From ancient times, England's lush pasture has nurtured superb livestock and a plentiful supply of dairy produce. The agricultural revolution from the late seventeenth century onwards led to an ever-greater supply of butter and cream. Foreign visitors marvelled at our profligate use of butter. We cared little for such opinions and relished our buttery pastries, cream-enriched fruit pies and flavoured milk puddings. As culinary technology developed with the creation of whisks, cake rings and oven ranges, so our baking expanded to encompass exquisite whisked sponges and fragile biscuits. We became famous for our superb tarts, cakes and puddings.

All of which takes me back to the contents of your fridge. Since dairy products are used in so many of our baking recipes, it is worth looking at them afresh. Have you compared the flavour of different brands of butter or thought about how eggs vary from one producer to another? Butter can differ enormously according to how it is made. The texture, colour

ABOVE LEFT The dairy at Berrington Hall, Herefordshire, unchanged since the 1780s.

ABOVE RIGHT Cool white tiles in the dairy scullery at Uppark, West Sussex.

and flavour of eggs will reflect the breed and diet of the chicken. Even milk changes throughout the year. Organic unhomogenised milk, for example, becomes more creamy and fragrant in the summer when the cows are grazing on grass. When the cows start eating silage in the winter, organic cream develops a more intense, almost acidic taste. Given that a simple recipe such as baked custard is primarily made from eggs, milk and cream, the better their flavour, the better the dish.

The best way to test such ingredients is to eat them plainly. Sip milk, lick a spoonful of cream, spread butter on bread, fry an egg. It will open your eyes to new culinary possibilities as you gain a greater understanding of the true taste and character of your chosen produce.

Take it one step further and search out local ingredients. If they're good, you could start to explore the idea of creating food that is directly linked to the landscape. What dishes might you cook to reflect your surroundings? The elderflower and gooseberry curd cake on page 44, for example, captures the feeling of my childhood on the North Downs of rural Surrey, of hot summers with the hens clucking under the gooseberry bushes.

ABOVE LEFT Tiles dating from around 1775 in the dairy at Hanbury Hall, Worcestershire.

ABOVE RIGHT The texture, colour and flavour of eggs will reflect the breed and diet of the chicken.

A GUIDE TO
DAIRY PRODUCE

BUTTER

Butter was once a mainstay of British cooking and its flavour still characterises many of our baked dishes. Today, most baking recipes recommend using unsalted butter as this allows greater control of the final taste. Most European butters are 'ripened' by the introduction of a lactic, acid-producing bacterial culture, which gives them a delicate sour note such as you find in French butter. British butter is usually made from 'unripened' churned cream. American cookbooks often call this 'sweet butter' as it is less acidic than 'ripened' butters. It is worth tasting different butters within your price range, as they can vary considerably in flavour.

Since butter absorbs flavours, it should always be stored carefully wrapped in the fridge. It freezes well. When a recipe requires the butter to be creamed, weigh out the specified amount of butter and let it come up to room temperature.

EGGS

The keen cook can choose from a wide variety of eggs, ranging from organic hens' eggs to those from different types of fowl such as bantams and ducks. In this book, I've used medium-sized organic hens' eggs unless otherwise specified. Duck eggs are good for custards, but their whites when whisked form smaller bubbles than hens' eggs, which give cakes and soufflés a denser texture.

It's sensible to use British-laid eggs. Look for the British Lion mark as this guarantees a strict code of hygiene and the hens are vaccinated against *Salmonella enteritidis*.

All eggs should be stored in the fridge at below 4°C/40°F as this lessens the risk of food poisoning. Ideally, store them on a shelf rather than in the fridge door as agitation thins the white. Separated egg whites should be covered and stored in the fridge for up to 3 weeks. Drop a little water on to separated egg yolks to prevent a skin from forming, then cover and store in the fridge for up to 3 days.

For the best results when baking, bring the eggs up to room temperature before using. This reduces the risk of them curdling (meaning that the mixture separates) when mixed with other ingredients.

If you're whisking egg whites, don't add any salt as it increases the whipping time and reduces the stability of the foam. Once whisked, fold them carefully into other mixtures to help maintain their fluffiness.

CREAM

In Britain, single cream has a fat content of 18 per cent, whipping cream has 36 per cent and double cream has 48 per cent. I have to admit that I have a weakness for using double cream in my recipes, mainly because it is so easy to cook with and it gives a luscious texture to baked custards and tart fillings, both sweet and savoury. The lower the fat content, the lighter, more watery the texture of the set. Extra-thick cream has been stabilised to make it spoonable without whipping, and is not used in baking recipes.

MILK

I love British organic unhomogenised whole (full-fat) milk as it has a wonderful sweet flavour and a lovely natural texture. Homogenisation breaks up the fat molecules in milk and disperses them evenly throughout the milk, which gives it a more creamy texture.

Whole (full-fat) milk has a fat content of 3.5 per cent, while semi-skimmed contains about 1.5–1.8 per cent. The latter can be used in place of whole milk in most recipes, but it won't have as rich a flavour. Skimmed milk has a fat content of 0.3 per cent and much less flavour.

Milk has a tendency to curdle (split into little lumps and runny liquid) when it comes into contact with acidic ingredients. One of the best ways to avoid this is to scald it by heating to just below boiling point. At this temperature, little bubbles form around the edge of the pan and the milk starts to steam. Never boil milk – it tastes horrid.

SOURED CREAM

Soured cream is made by adding a lactic-acid-producing bacteria to single cream, which thickens it and makes it taste deliciously tart. Perfect for cheesecakes.

CRÈME FRAÎCHE

It doesn't sound very English, but crème fraîche has become a much-loved British ingredient. It is a mildly sour-tasting bacterially cultured cream. The full-fat version is made from double cream and can be treated in the same way. It will thin slightly when first stirred, but can be whipped or even boiled. Low-fat crème fraîche may split when heated.

BUTTERMILK

Originally, buttermilk was the liquid left after the cream had been churned to make butter. Today, it is made by introducing a culture to low-fat milk to thicken it slightly. It tastes similar to yoghurt, but only has 2 per cent fat. Buttermilk is mainly used in baking recipes that need acidity to help them rise, such as soda bread and some scones. Its acidity is combined with the alkaline bicarbonate of soda to produce bubbles of carbon dioxide that puff the mix up.

NATURAL YOGHURT

This is made by fermenting milk with lactic-acid-producing bacteria and can be used instead of buttermilk or soured milk in baking recipes. Its fat content ranges from 2 per cent (low fat) to 10.2 per cent (Greek yoghurt).

BUTTERY CAKES
& WHISKED SPONGES

Cakes have a very special place in British culture. Over the centuries, we have developed a wide range of delicious recipes, many of which evolved as a result of having a rich supply of butter and eggs at our fingertips. This section introduces some classic examples of different cake-making methods that depend on eggs, and in some cases butter, to create their delicate texture.

Every cake-maker has a sense of pleasure as they assemble their ingredients. Somehow, it's amazing that a fragile whisked sponge can be created from the equal weight of eggs, sugar and flour. Yet the power of the egg as a raising agent did not become fully appreciated until the eighteenth century, after the invention of the wooden or tin baking hoop at the end of the seventeenth century. Up until then, British cakes were a splendiferous form of enriched bread. They were made from a hearty mixture of dried fruit, spice, sugar or honey, and cream or butter. The heavy dough was further enriched with eggs, but risen by ale yeast and baked like a round loaf in a cool bread oven. The spiced yule bread on page 286 is a good example.

Once English cooks could contain their cake batter within buttered and papered moulds, myriad new recipes began to appear. Butter and sugar were beaten together until fluffy; eggs, both whole and separated, were beaten to incorporate air bubbles; sometimes extra whisked egg whites were folded into the batter just before baking. Delicate, crumbly cakes made their appearance. By the mid-eighteenth century, recipes for both yeast-risen and egg-risen cakes could be found in books such as Mrs Raffald's *The Experienced English Housekeeper* (1769).

However, it was Thomas Robinson's invention of the kitchen range in 1780 that ultimately popularised cake-baking. His range allowed small households to have an oven in their

home, making cake-baking accessible to the middle classes. Alfred Bird's invention of baking powder (see page 96) in 1843 ensured that even less able cooks could feel confident about producing well-risen cakes.

Today, British cake-making can be divided into three main methods: melting, creaming and whisking. Each method is designed to get air into a cake. The easiest is the 'melting' method, as used for date and walnut tea-bread on page 104. Butter and sugar are melted together, cooled slightly and then combined with a raising agent to produce a cake. This method usually includes eggs.

The 'creaming' method depends on beating together butter and sugar to incorporate air into the mixture, before folding in beaten eggs, followed by flour, usually self-raising. The Victoria sponge on page 33 is a classic example. A lighter variation of this method is to beat egg yolks into the creamed butter, then fold in the flour, followed by the whisked egg whites.

The 'whisking' method incorporates air into the cake mixture by whisking eggs and sugar together until they form a thick foam. Plain flour can then be folded in, as with strawberry cream cake on page 34. This type of whisked sponge is best eaten on the day it's baked as it contains no fat and quickly becomes dry. A variation of this is the génoise sponge, in which cool melted butter and plain flour are folded into the egg and sugar mixture to make a richer whisked sponge, for example the praline butter génoise on page 38.

Génoise is my favourite type of sponge, but it is often reputed to be difficult to make. It needs a gentle hand but will reward the cook with an exquisite sponge.

There are, of course, as many permutations of these methods as there are cake recipes. You'll find many more recipes throughout this book.

LEMON VICTORIA SANDWICH

A Victoria sandwich cake is made from equal weights of eggs, butter, sugar and self-raising flour. A medium egg in its shell weighs 55g/2oz; so if you have different sized eggs, adjust the weight of the other ingredients accordingly. If you don't have self-raising flour, add ¼ teaspoon baking powder to every 55g/2oz plain white flour. Traditionally, the sponge is unflavoured and filled with raspberry jam or lemon curd; this is a more luxurious, buttery lemon version.

SERVES 8

VICTORIA SPONGE CAKE
225g/8oz butter, softened
225g/8oz caster sugar
finely grated zest and juice of 4 lemons
4 medium eggs
225g/8oz self-raising flour, sifted
6 tablespoons milk

LEMON BUTTER CREAM
finely grated zest and juice of 3 lemons
170g/6oz butter, softened
125g/4½ oz icing sugar, sifted

DECORATION
sugared primroses (see page 133) and/or ½ lemon

1 Preheat the oven to fan 170°C/gas 4. Lightly oil two 18cm/7in sandwich tins. Line the base of each with baking parchment.

2 To make the sponge cake, cream the softened butter and sugar together in a large bowl, using a wooden spoon or electric whisk, until pale and fluffy. Add the grated lemon zest.

3 Break the eggs into a jug, roughly beat with a fork and whisk a little at a time into the creamed butter. If the mixture begins to curdle, add 2 tablespoons flour. Once all the eggs have been whisked into the mixture, use a flat metal spoon to gently fold in the remaining flour in three batches. Loosen the mixture with 2 tablespoons lemon juice and 6 tablespoons milk, so that the mixture drops off the spoon in soft blobs.

4 Quickly divide the mixture between the tins and smooth the tops. Bake for about 20 minutes or until the cakes are well risen, golden brown and spring back when lightly pressed with a fingertip.

5 Place on a wire rack for 5 minutes. Then, using a knife, gently loosen the sides of each cake from its tin. Turn out, peel off the baking paper, and leave to cool.

6 To make the lemon butter cream, place the lemon zest, butter and icing sugar in a mixing bowl. Using an electric whisk, beat thoroughly until light and fluffy. Then gradually whisk in 4½ tablespoons lemon juice.

7 Once the cakes are cold, spread a third of the butter cream on one of the cakes. Sandwich the other cake on top, baked-side up. Spread another third of the cream on the top and the remaining third around the sides of the cake. Chill for 30 minutes to set the butter cream.

8 Decorate with sugared primroses or cut a lemon in half lengthways, and then cut into thin slices.

STRAWBERRY CREAM CAKE

This cake is the picture of summer if you place a freshly opened rose on its sugary top. Perfect for June birthdays. As it is a whisked sponge, and contains no fat, it is best eaten on the day it's baked. The sponge freezes well and makes a wonderful trifle.

SERVES 8

WHISKED SPONGE
85g/3oz caster sugar, plus extra for dusting
85g/3oz plain flour, sifted, plus extra for dusting
pinch of salt
3 medium eggs

1 Preheat the oven to fan 170°C/gas 4. Lightly oil two 18cm/7in cake tins. Line the base with baking parchment and lightly oil. Dust the sides of each tin with caster sugar and then with flour.

2 Sift the flour and salt together and set aside. Place the eggs and 85g/3oz sugar in a large bowl. If you have an electric whisk, beat until the mixture is pale and thick and leaves a trail when you lift the whisk. If you're whisking by hand, place the bowl over a pan of just-boiled water (off the heat); whisk until it is pale and thick, then remove from the pan and continue to whisk until cool.

3 Tip the flour over the surface of the whisked egg mixture and, using a flat metal spoon, gently fold the flour into the mixture. Divide between the two tins and bake for 20 minutes or until golden. Test by lightly pressing the cake with your fingertip: it will spring back if cooked.

STRAWBERRY FILLING
310g/11oz strawberries
1 tablespoon kirsch
2 tablespoons caster sugar
225ml/8fl oz double cream

4 Leave the cakes in their tins on a wire rack for 5 minutes. Turn out the cakes and peel off the baking paper. Dust the top of one cake (baked-side up) with caster sugar. Leave until cold.

5 Meanwhile, hull, halve and slice the strawberries. Toss with the kirsch and 2 tablespoons caster sugar.

6 Once the cakes are cold, whip the cream until it forms soft peaks. Fold in the strawberry mixture. Spread over the bottom sponge, leaving a clear edge for the cream to squeeze into when you add the top. Gently squash on the sugared top and add a further dusting of caster sugar.

SEVILLE ORANGE CRUNCH CAKE

This drizzle cake is made by what is often called the 'creaming' method. The wet, sugary topping enhances its moist, buttery texture. Seville oranges are normally sold in the last three weeks of January. They freeze well, as does their juice. If juicing, grate the zest first. The best way to freeze the zest is to beat it into measured portions of butter and then freeze. If you don't have access to Seville oranges, use a normal 'sweet' orange instead.

SERVES 8

115g/4oz butter, softened
170g/6oz caster sugar
finely grated zest and juice of 1 Seville orange
finely grated zest and juice of 1 lemon

3 medium eggs, beaten
170g/6oz self-raising flour, sifted
115g/4oz granulated sugar

1 Preheat the oven to fan 180°C/gas 5. Lightly oil an 18cm/7in cake tin. Line the base with baking parchment.

2 In a large bowl, beat the butter, caster sugar and citrus zests together vigorously until pale and fluffy. Using a metal spoon, fold in one-third of the eggs, followed by one-third of the flour. Repeat until all the eggs and flour are incorporated, then fold in 2 tablespoons Seville orange juice and 2 tablespoons lemon juice, and spoon the mixture into the prepared cake tin. Level the surface and bake for about 35 minutes or until the cake springs back when lightly pressed and a skewer inserted into the cake comes out clean.

3 Remove the cake from the oven and place on a wire rack. Quickly mix the remaining citrus juice with the granulated sugar and pour evenly over the piping-hot surface of the cake. Don't mix the citrus juice and granulated sugar until you've taken the cake out of the oven. Otherwise, the sugar will dissolve and you won't get a lovely crunch.

4 Leave until cool enough to handle, then remove the cake from its tin and leave to cool on a wire rack. When cold, peel off the baking paper.

COFFEE CREAM SWISS ROLL

This is an ultra-sugary, rainy afternoon treat. If you want to fill your Swiss roll with jam instead of coffee butter cream, sieve 3 tablespoons of good raspberry or strawberry jam then, using a palette knife, spread it on to the still-warm sponge and roll up.

SERVES 8

WHISKED SPONGE
85g/3oz caster sugar, plus extra for dusting
85g/3oz plain flour, sifted, plus extra for dusting
pinch of salt
3 medium eggs

COFFEE BUTTER CREAM
1½ tablespoons instant coffee granules
225g/8oz butter, softened
170g/6oz icing sugar, sifted

1 Preheat the oven to fan 170°C/gas 4. Cut a piece of baking parchment slightly larger than a 20 x 30cm/8 x 12in Swiss roll tin. Lightly oil the tin. Fold each edge of the parchment so that it forms a 2.5cm/1in rim. Press the paper into the tin to fit neatly and line the sides. Lightly brush the paper with oil, dust with caster sugar and then with flour.

2 Sift the flour and salt together and set aside. Place the eggs and 85g/3oz sugar in a large bowl. If you have an electric whisk, beat until the mixture is pale and thick and leaves a trail when you lift the whisk. If you're whisking by hand, place the bowl over a pan of just-boiled water (off the heat); whisk until it is pale and thick, then remove from the pan and continue to whisk until cool.

3 Tip the flour over the surface of the whisked egg mixture and, using a flat metal spoon, gently fold the flour into the mixture. Spoon into the prepared tin and spread evenly. Bake for 12–15 minutes or until golden and risen. Cool for 15 minutes.

4 Place a sheet of baking parchment on the work surface and sprinkle evenly with caster sugar. Loosen the edge of the sponge with a knife, then gently invert the sponge on to the sugared paper. Very carefully, peel away the baking paper. If necessary, trim the edges of the cake. To prevent the sponge from cracking, cover it with another sheet of baking parchment and very gently roll it up from the shorter side, using the paper underneath the cake to help you roll.

5 To make the coffee butter cream, dissolve the coffee granules in 1 tablespoon boiling water. Place the butter and icing sugar in a mixing bowl. Beat thoroughly using an electric whisk until pale and fluffy, then whisk in the coffee. Transfer to a bowl and keep at room temperature.

6 The Swiss roll must be cool before you add the butter cream. Once cool, carefully unroll. Using a palette knife, gently spread with the coffee butter cream and roll up again. Place on a serving plate, lightly cover and chill for 30 minutes to firm up the butter cream.

PRALINE BUTTER GÉNOISE

The génoise sponge has a reputation for being tricky to make. It contains melted butter, which creates a softer crumb and moister texture than fatless whisked sponges. Success depends on whisking the eggs and sugar to a billowing foam that will hold a trail, before lightly folding in the butter and then the flour. It requires a flat metal spoon, a light hand and confidence to ensure that you don't deflate the eggs or create lumps of raw flour as you fold.

Once filled, you can keep the cake in the fridge for up to 3 days. The unfilled cake can be frozen for up to a month.

SERVES 8

GÉNOISE SPONGE
115g/4oz plain flour, sifted, plus extra for dusting
pinch of salt
4 medium eggs
115g/4oz caster sugar
55g/2oz butter, melted and cooled

PRALINE BUTTER CREAM
55g/2oz blanched whole almonds
55g/2oz blanched hazelnuts
115g/4oz granulated sugar
225g/8oz butter, softened
30g/1oz icing sugar
pinch of salt (optional)

1 Preheat the oven to fan 170°C/gas 4. Lightly oil two 18cm/7in sandwich tins. Line with baking parchment. Lightly oil and then dust with flour. Sift the flour and salt together and set aside.

2 Choose a large bowl that will fit over a saucepan. Pour some just-boiled water into the saucepan, but take care that it doesn't touch the bowl. Put the eggs and sugar in the bowl and set over the pan (off the heat). Whisk for 5 minutes with a hand-held electric whisk until the mixture has doubled in volume to form a thick, pale foam that leaves a trail for about 5 seconds when you lift the whisk. The mixture will be slightly warm.

3 Remove the bowl from the hot water and continue to beat until the mixture cools to room temperature. Pour the cool melted butter around the edge of the bowl and, using a metal spoon, gently fold it in.

4 Immediately sift half the flour over the surface, and partially fold it in with a few gentle folds. Repeat with the remaining flour, lightly folding until all the flour is incorporated into the mixture. Divide the mixture between the cake tins. Bake for 20 minutes or until the cake has shrunk away from the rim of the tin and springs back when lightly pressed.

5 Turn the cakes upside down on a wire rack and remove the tins. Leave until cold before peeling off the baking paper. If you wish, you can wrap and freeze the sponge at this stage.

6 To make the praline butter cream, lightly oil a non-stick baking sheet. Place the almonds, hazelnuts and granulated sugar in a wide, heavy-bottomed saucepan. Set over a low heat and stir occasionally until the sugar has melted and is beginning to caramelise. Continue to cook until it turns a clear golden brown. Tip on to the oiled sheet and leave until cold and set. Roughly break up the mixture and tip into a food processor. Grind to a fine powder, then tip the praline into a bowl.

7 Put the butter and icing sugar into the food processor. Whiz until fluffy, then add the praline and, if you wish, a pinch of salt to taste. Briefly process then transfer to a bowl and mix thoroughly.

8 Using a palette knife, spread a little of the soft praline butter cream over the bottom sponge. Gently press the other sponge on top (baked-side up), then spread the remaining butter cream over the top and sides of the cake and carefully smooth with a palette knife. Chill for 30 minutes or until the butter cream is set.

ORANGE ALMOND CAKE ⓖⓕ

In 1968, in her wonderful *A Book of Middle Eastern Food*, Claudia Roden introduced the British to a Sephardic cake made from almonds and boiled oranges. Little did she realise that this moist cake would become a favourite amongst British cake-bakers. As it happens, it is also a good example of a gluten-free whisked sponge. This National Trust version comes from Bateman's, Rudyard Kipling's home in Burwash in the Sussex Weald.

SERVES 10

2 organic oranges (about 400g/14oz)
1 organic lemon
6 medium eggs

225g/8oz caster sugar
225g/8oz ground almonds
4 teaspoons baking powder (gluten-free)

1 Place the oranges and lemon in a large pan. Cover with cold water and bring to the boil. Simmer for 2 hours, then drain and leave until cool. Cut each fruit in half and remove the pips. Purée to a pulp in a food processor and then transfer to a very large bowl.

2 Preheat the oven to fan 180°C/gas 5. Lightly oil a 23cm/9in spring-form cake tin. Line the base with baking parchment. You can use a 22cm/8½ in tin, but it will take slightly longer to cook.

3 In a large bowl, whisk together the eggs and caster sugar until they form a thick, pale foam that leaves a trail for a few seconds when you lift the whisk.

4 Mix together the almonds and baking powder. Once thoroughly mixed, stir them into the cold pulped fruit. Using a flat metal spoon, gently fold in a couple of large spoonfuls of the egg and sugar mixture into the pulped oranges to loosen the mixture, then slowly fold in the remaining egg mixture.

5 Quickly tip into the cake tin and bake for 30 minutes. Check the cake and, if the top is colouring too quickly, lightly cover with foil to prevent it from burning or colouring further. Bake for a further 45–60 minutes (depending on the size of your cake tin: the deeper 22cm/8½ in cake will take nearer 60 minutes). After 45 minutes, test by inserting a skewer into the centre of the cake: if it comes out clean, the cake is cooked.

6 Leave to cool in its tin on a wire rack for 5 minutes or until cool, then remove from the tin.

CURDS & ...

The origins of lemon curd are shrouded in mystery. In *Traditional Foods of Britain* (2004), Laura Mason suggests that lemon curd might have developed from an eighteenth-century English dish called transparent pudding – a tart filled with a glossy curd of eggs, butter and sugar that was flavoured with nutmeg. By the nineteenth century, transparent pudding had evolved into tarts with different flavoured curd fillings, although, at that time, their filling was called lemon or orange cheese rather than curd. By 1861, Mrs Beeton instructs the cook that the lemon cheese filling can be made and stored in advance.

However, in the 1970s, with the British fashion for self-sufficiency, cooks began to experiment with other types of fruit curd such as rhubarb, and gooseberry. Lemon juice was added to the sweeter fruit combinations, such as blackberry.

Enthusiastic bakers found fruit curds an invaluable addition to their repertoire. Their sweet-sour taste, gooey consistency and bright colour enhanced cakes, tarts and meringues. The popularity of passion fruit curd in the 1990s ensured that curds remained fashionable. Who could resist such exotic notes in a soft meringue roulade, Victoria sponge or Swiss roll?

Most fruit curd recipes are based on the proportions for lemon curd: the juice and zest of 4 lemons, 4 strained eggs, 115g/4oz butter and 340g/12oz caster sugar. So, for example, as one lemon yields 50ml/scant 2fl oz juice, you should use about 200ml/7fl oz passion fruit juice to four eggs. It is then easy to adjust a recipe to suit your chosen fruit. Lime juice is more acidic than lemon, so less is needed. It is important to ensure that the curd only thickens enough to coat the back of the spoon, as it will thicken further as it cools. Fruit curd can be stored in the fridge for up to 3 weeks.

ELDERFLOWER AND GOOSEBERRY CURD CAKE

Elderflowers and gooseberries taste wonderful together. There is just a hint of elderflower in this rustic cake. You will need to make the curd a day ahead: it thickens as it cools. Some supermarkets and independent drinks shops sell St-Germain elderflower liqueur.

SERVES 8

génoise sponge (see page 38)

GOOSEBERRY CURD
340g/12oz gooseberries, topped and tailed
juice of ½ lemon
1 medium egg
85g/3oz caster sugar
30g/1oz butter

ELDERFLOWER ICING
200g/7oz icing sugar
2½ tablespoons St-Germain elderflower liqueur
2 tablespoons lemon juice

1 A day in advance, make the gooseberry curd. Place the gooseberries in a non-corrosive saucepan with the lemon juice, cover and set over a low heat. Once the gooseberries start to release some juice, increase the heat slightly and simmer gently for 10 minutes or until they've collapsed and are swimming in juice. Liquidise and push through a fine sieve. Measure 100ml/3½ fl oz of the gooseberry purée. The remainder can be used in a fool.

2 Strain the egg into a saucepan. Mix in the gooseberry purée, sugar and butter. Set over a low heat. Stir until the butter has melted and the mixture begins to coat the back of the spoon – this will take a good 10 minutes. Don't worry if you think it looks too runny, it will thicken as it cools. Transfer to a clean container, cover and chill.

3 The next day, bake your génoise sponge, following steps 1–5 on page 38. Sandwich the two cakes together with the gooseberry curd, taking care to leave the baked side up on the top for the icing.

4 To make the elderflower icing, sift the icing sugar into a bowl. Using a wooden spoon, stir the elderflower liqueur and lemon juice into the sugar until it forms a thick, smooth icing. Pour on to the centre of the cake and, using a wet palette knife, gently smooth out to evenly cover the top of the cake, letting it dribble over the edges of the cake. Leave until set and then transfer to a clean plate. This cake keeps well in the fridge for up to 3 days – lightly cover with clingfilm. The flavours develop in a delicious way.

LIME CURD TARTS

This recipe comes from Geraldene Holt's *The National Trust Book of Tuck Box Treats* (1987). She originally devised the recipe for her cake stall at Tiverton Market in Devon. One hundred and fifty years ago, Mrs Beeton would have recognised it as a lime cheesecake rather than a curd tart. The term 'cheese' was used to refer to a thick preserve such as damson cheese. Thus, lemon curd was called lemon cheese. These tarts have a delicious fresh flavour.

MAKES 18 TARTS

225g/8oz rich shortcrust pastry (see page 82)
finely grated zest and strained juice of 2 limes
2 large eggs, beaten and strained

85g/3oz caster sugar
55g/2oz butter, melted and cooled

1 Preheat the oven fan 190°C/gas 6. Lightly grease 18 patty tins (see bun tray, page 15).

2 Make a sweetened version of the rich shortcrust pasty on page 82. Then roll out the pastry thinly. Using a 7.5cm/3in diameter fluted pastry cutter, stamp out 18 pastry circles and line the patty tins. Prick the bottom of each with a fork, line with greaseproof paper, and fill with baking beans. Chill for 30 minutes.

3 Bake the pastry cases for 6–7 minutes, until the pastry is set and is starting to change colour at the edge. Remove from the oven, remove the paper and baking beans, and reduce the oven temperature to fan 170°C/gas 4.

4 Put the lime zest and juice in a bowl. Beat in the strained eggs, sugar and melted butter. Spoon into the pastry cases and bake for 5 minutes or until the filling is set. Cool slightly and transfer the tarts to a wire rack to cool.

ORANGE AND LEMON CURD PUDDING

It might sound contradictory to include little steamed puddings in a baking book, but the best way to cook them is in the oven. The luscious lemon curd sauce can be kept warm in a Thermos flask. The pudding mixture makes seven puddings – just in case!

SERVES 7

170g/6oz butter, plus extra for greasing
170g/6oz caster sugar
finely grated zest and juice of 2 small oranges
finely grated zest and juice of 1 lemon
3 medium eggs
170g/6oz self-raising flour, sifted
pinch of salt

55g/2oz white breadcrumbs
85g/3oz chopped mixed peel

LEMON CURD SAUCE
finely grated zest and juice of 2 large lemons
115g/4oz butter, softened
170g/6oz caster sugar
2 medium eggs, lightly beaten

1 Take seven 150ml/5fl oz pudding basins. Using a basin bottom as a template, draw seven circles on some baking parchment. Use the top of a basin to draw seven more circles, then cut out all the circles. Liberally butter the basins, then line the basin bottoms with small discs. Cut seven squares of foil large enough to be fitted over their tops. Preheat the oven to fan 220°C/gas 8.

2 In a bowl, beat together the butter and sugar with the orange and lemon zest until light and fluffy. Add a tablespoon of lemon juice, followed by the eggs. Stir in the flour and salt, followed by the breadcrumbs, mixed peel, the remaining lemon juice and enough orange juice for the batter to form a soft dropping consistency.

3 Fill each pudding basin two-thirds full. Cover with a disc of parchment and then a square of foil, tucking the foil around the rim of the basin to neatly seal. Repeat with the remaining basins. Place in a roasting pan. Pour in enough boiling water to come over halfway up the sides of the basins. Cover the pan with foil and cook in the oven for 1 hour.

4 Meanwhile, make the lemon curd sauce. Choose a bowl that will fit neatly over a saucepan. Place the lemon zest and juice in the bowl with the butter and sugar. Strain the eggs through a sieve into the bowl and place the bowl over a pan of simmering water. Stir continuously until the butter has melted and the mixture has thickened enough to coat the back of a spoon. Pour into a warmed Thermos flask and seal until it is needed.

5 Remove the puddings from the oven. Rest for 5 minutes. The sponge will shrink back slightly, making it easy to turn out. Turn out the hot puddings, removing the baking paper. Serve liberally drizzled with the warm lemon curd sauce.

BLACKCURRANT MERINGUE PIE

Fruit curds for meringue pies are usually thickened with cornflour to ensure that the eggs in the curd don't split when baked. As cornflour cooks, it turns the fruit curd opaque (see photograph). It needs to be thoroughly cooked before adding the eggs as it has a distinctive 'floury' texture when partially cooked. However, when first testing this recipe, I accidentally added arrowroot instead of cornflower. Arrowroot becomes translucent as it cooks and sets to a more jelly-like consistency, which you either love or hate: I loved it.

SERVES 6

225g/8oz shortcrust pastry (see page 80)

BLACKCURRANT FILLING
750g/1lb 10oz blackcurrants
170g/6oz caster sugar
60g/2¼ oz cornflour or 55g/2oz arrowroot

55g/2oz butter, diced
3 medium egg yolks, strained

MERINGUE TOPPING
3 medium egg whites
170g/6oz caster sugar

1 Roll out the pastry and line a 20cm/8in tarl tin with a removable base. Prick the pastry with a fork, line with greaseproof paper and fill with baking beans. Chill for 30 minutes. Preheat the oven to fan 180°C/gas 5.

2 Bake the pastry case for 15 minutes. Remove the paper and beans and bake for a further 5 minutes, or until the pastry has become dry but not coloured. Remove from the oven and reduce the oven temperature to fan 140°C/gas 2.

3 To make the filling, put the blackcurrants in a non-corrosive saucepan with 3 tablespoons water. Cover and set over a medium-low heat. When the currants begin to release some juice, simmer for 20 minutes or until they're meltingly soft. Push through a sieve and measure out about 450ml/16fl oz blackcurrant purée.

4 Place the sugar and cornflour (or arrowroot) in a non-corrosive saucepan. Using a wooden spoon, slowly stir in the blackcurrant purée so that it forms a smooth paste. Set over a medium heat and stir continuously for 5 minutes or until the mixture is bubbling, thick and translucent – make sure it no longer tastes of raw cornflour (or arrowroot). Remove from the heat and beat in the butter, followed by the egg yolks. Spoon the mixture into the pastry case.

5 To make the meringue topping, whisk the egg whites in a clean bowl until they form stiff peaks. Add 85g/3oz of the caster sugar and continue to whisk, gradually adding the remaining sugar. Continue to whisk until it forms soft glossy peaks. Gently spread the meringue over the tart so that it touches the pastry rim and seals in the gooey filling. You can make it spiky or smooth.

6 Return the pie to the oven and bake for 30 minutes or until the meringue has set with a crisp, very lightly browned crust. The curd becomes firmer as it cools. If serving the next day, store uncovered on the top shelf of the fridge.

CUSTARD TARTS & CHEESECAKES

Our taste for custard tarts and cheesecakes dates back to at least the fifteenth century. During the summer months, when soft curd cheeses, eggs and cream were plentiful, the tables of the wealthy would be laden with rich custard tarts and curd cheese tarts. The latter are now known as cheesecakes. Such dishes were popular on meatless days, such as 'fish' Wednesdays, as dairy produce, including eggs, was considered to be white meat and therefore suitable for fast days when red meat was forbidden.

Although we commonly associate custard tarts and cheesecakes with cow's milk, it is likely that sheep's milk was used in much of England until the late seventeenth century, when farming techniques changed and cows became more widespread. You might like to try different milks in your baking. For example, the vanilla cheesecake on page 56 uses a lemony goat's curd cheese. You will find another cheesecake recipe, with hazelnut brittle, on page 251.

A perfectly baked custard tart should have a smooth creamy filling and crisp buttery pastry. The pastry helps protect the fragile filling from the dry oven heat. Some recipes use cornflour, breadcrumbs or ground almonds to stabilise the custard. As a general rule, custard tarts and cheesecakes are best baked gently at around fan 140°C/gas 2 to ensure that they set to a creamy consistency and don't crack on their tops.

A FINE CUSTARD TART

This recipe is based on an Eliza Acton recipe from her 1855 edition of *Modern Cookery for Private Families*. It remains an exceptional classic custard tart. Incidentally, you can use the spare egg whites in a fruit soufflé such as that on page 214 or in the soft hazelnut macaroons on page 252.

SERVES 8

225g/8oz shortcrust pastry (see page 80)
425ml/15fl oz full-fat milk
pinch of salt
85g/3oz granulated sugar
finely pared zest of 1 lemon

2 medium eggs
3 medium egg yolks
150ml/5fl oz double cream
2 tablespoons brandy
freshly grated nutmeg

1 Preheat the oven to fan 180°C/gas 5. Roll out the pastry and line a 23cm/9in china quiche dish or a tart tin with a removable base. If there are any holes in your pastry, patch them up with little pieces of pastry. You don't want the custard to leak out. Prick the pastry with a fork, line with greaseproof paper, and fill with baking beans. Chill for 30 minutes.

2 Bake the pastry case for 10 minutes, remove the paper and beans, and bake for a further 8–10 minutes or until it no longer looks raw. Remove from the oven and reduce the oven temperature to fan 140°C/gas 2.

3 Put the milk, salt, sugar and lemon zest in a saucepan. Set over a medium heat and stir until the sugar has dissolved, then bring up to the boil and remove from the heat.

4 Put the eggs and egg yolks in a mixing bowl. Beat thoroughly and then slowly stir in the hot milk. Strain through a sieve into a large jug. Mix in the cream and brandy and pour the mixture into the pastry case. Quickly grate some nutmeg over the top and bake for 30–40 minutes or until just set. It should be golden and slightly puffed up, with a faint wobble. Leave to cool in its dish or tin. If baked in a tin, remove from the tin when the tart is cold and place on a serving plate. Serve at room temperature.

CINNAMON PUMPKIN PIE

Custard tarts come in many guises, including this delicately flavoured pumpkin pie, which I've adapted from my 1909 edition of *Mrs Beeton's Every-day Cookery*. The terms 'pie' and 'tart' have always been interchangeable in Britain. You could use butternut squash in place of pumpkin. One small pumpkin will yield about 400g/14oz flesh.

SERVES 6

225g/8oz rich shortcrust pastry (see page 80)
400g/14oz peeled, deseeded pumpkin flesh
200ml/7fl oz water
85g/3oz caster sugar
finely grated zest of 2 lemons

3 tablespoons dry sherry
1 teaspoon ground cinnamon
5 medium egg yolks
150ml/5fl oz double cream
icing sugar for dusting

1 Roll out the pastry and line a 20cm/8in tart tin with a removable base or a china quiche dish. If there are any holes in your pastry, patch them up with little pieces of pastry – you don't want the custard to leak out. Prick the pastry with a fork, line with greaseproof paper and baking beans. Chill for 30 minutes. Preheat the oven to fan 180°C/gas 5.

2 Meanwhile, roughly chop the pumpkin flesh and put in a saucepan with the water. Cover, bring to the boil, then simmer for about 20 minutes or until the pumpkin is very soft and the water has evaporated. The final mixture should be quite dry. Purée the pumpkin.

3 Bake the pastry case for 10 minutes, then remove the paper and beans and bake for a further 8–10 minutes or until the pastry no longer looks raw. Remove from the oven.

4 Mix the warm pumpkin purée with the sugar, lemon zest, sherry and cinnamon. Beat the egg yolks and cream together and stir into the pumpkin mixture. Pour into the pastry case. Bake for 30 minutes or until just set, with a slight wobble. If baked in a tin, remove gently and serve warm or cold, dusted with icing sugar.

YORKSHIRE CURD TART

Fashions come and go with food. Four hundred years ago, this curd tart, a type of cheesecake, might have been eaten across the country; today, you will only find it sold in Yorkshire. Time to revive such an exquisite recipe.

I used a full-fat fromage frais when testing this recipe as curd cheese is not always easy to find. Don't worry about the granular look of the raw cheese mixture – the finished tart should have a slightly granular texture.

SERVES 6

115g/4oz raisins or currants
3 tablespoons dark rum
225g/8oz lard shortcrust pastry (see page 82)
115g/4oz butter, softened
55g/2oz caster sugar
225g/8oz curd cheese or full-fat fromage frais

1 heaped tablespoon white breadcrumbs
2 medium eggs, well beaten
pinch of salt
freshly grated nutmeg
icing sugar for dusting

1 If you have time, soak the raisins or currants in the rum overnight.

2 Roll out the pastry and line a deep 20cm/8in tart tin with a removable base. Prick the pastry with a fork, line with greaseproof paper and baking beans. Chill for 30 minutes. Preheat the oven to fan 180°C/gas 5.

3 Bake the pastry case for 10 minutes, remove the paper and beans, and bake for a further 8–10 minutes or until it no longer looks raw.

4 While the pastry is cooking, make the filling. Beat the butter and caster sugar together until they're pale and fluffy, then beat in the curd cheese, followed by the breadcrumbs, raisins or currants, rum and eggs. Season to taste with salt and nutmeg.

5 As soon as the pastry is ready, pour the filling into the pastry case and return to the oven. Bake for 20–30 minutes or until flecked golden brown. Leave to cool. Once cold, gently remove from the tin. Serve dusted with icing sugar.

SOURED CREAM CHEESECAKE

Over the centuries British cheesecakes have changed. This light, lemony version reflects the modern style that is influenced by American-style baking – which in turn was influenced by Europe. Instead of the raspberries, you can serve this with any soft fruit. You will need to make this a day ahead.

SERVES 6

115g/4oz digestive biscuits
55g/2oz butter, melted
150g/5½ oz full-fat cottage cheese
185g/6½ oz full-fat cream cheese
150ml/5fl oz soured cream
finely grated zest of 1 lemon
freshly grated nutmeg

2 tablespoons cornflour
3 medium eggs, separated
85g/3oz caster sugar

TO SERVE
icing sugar for dusting
250g/9oz fresh raspberries

1 Preheat the oven to fan 140°C/gas 2. Lightly oil a 20cm/8in spring-form cake tin. Put the digestive biscuits in a plastic bag and crush with a rolling pin until they form fine crumbs. Mix into the melted butter. Press the crumbs firmly and evenly over the base of the tin. Chill in the fridge while you prepare the filling.

2 Push the cottage cheese through a sieve into a large mixing bowl. Add the cream cheese, soured cream, lemon zest and lots of nutmeg. Sift the cornflour over the mixture and beat thoroughly. Mix in the egg yolks and sugar.

3 Put the egg whites in a large, clean, dry bowl. Whisk until they form soft peaks. Using a large metal spoon, slowly fold the egg whites into the cream cheese mixture. Immediately pour the mixture on to the chilled biscuit base and place in the centre of the oven. Bake for 65 minutes without opening the oven door. Turn off the heat and leave to cool in the oven for a further 2 hours. Remove and leave until cold, then chill in the tin. Don't worry if the surface of the cheesecake forms cracks, it's so light it has a tendency to do this.

4 Once cold, run a knife around the edge of the cheesecake before gently unclipping the spring-form tin. Using a palette knife, carefully ease the cake off its metal base on to a plate. Loosely cover with foil and chill until needed. Serve dusted with icing sugar and piles of fresh raspberries.

VANILLA CHEESECAKE WITH (GF) SUGARED RED CURRANTS

This is an incredibly light and fragile cheesecake as it has no pastry base. Goat's curd is made by artisan producers and can be found in good cheese shops. It has a delicious lemony taste, but if you're unable to find any, you can use cow's milk curd cheese or full-fat fromage frais instead.

SERVES 6

450g/1lb goat's curd
¼ teaspoon vanilla extract
finely grated zest of 2 lemons
1¼ tablespoons cornflour
juice of 1½ lemons

4 medium eggs
115g/4oz caster sugar, plus extra for the
    red currants
340g/12oz red currants, washed

1 Preheat the oven to fan 180°C/gas 5. Lightly oil a 20cm/8in spring-form cake tin. Line the base and sides with baking parchment (see page 19 for instructions).

2 Place the goat's curd cheese in a large mixing bowl. Add the vanilla and lemon zest. Place the cornflour in a small bowl and mix in the lemon juice to form a smooth paste. Tip into the goat's curd cheese. Using a balloon whisk, gently whisk the ingredients together until they're just mixed through. Do not over-mix.

3 In a separate bowl, whisk together the eggs and caster sugar, then gradually whisk them into the curd cheese. Pour the mixture into the prepared tin and bake for 50 minutes or until golden brown. It should still tremble when it comes out of the oven, but it will set as it cools.

4 Once cold, remove the cheesecake from its tin and use the paper to help slide it onto a plate, using a palette knife. You can either leave the red currants on their stems or strip them, as you prefer. Just before serving, toss the red currants in lots of caster sugar and pile on top of the cheesecake.

BAKED CREAMS

At their simplest, baked creams (custards) are made with eggs, sugar and milk and/or cream. They can be made with whole eggs or egg yolks or both. The more eggs in proportion to milk, the thicker the set of the baked custard, and the more egg white in the mixture, the more rubbery the set. The ratio for the perfect set is said to be 1 egg and 1 yolk to a splash over 70ml/2½ fl oz full-fat milk and 70ml/2½ fl oz double cream. Too much sugar will inhibit their ability to set.

You can flavour baked creams by infusing the milk or cream with spices such as cinnamon, cardamom, saffron and vanilla, as well as herbs, for example bay or rosemary. Coffee, tea or chocolate also taste delicious. You can even combine the cream custard with puréed fruit. Elsewhere in this book, you will find apricot creams (page 189) and spiced tea creams (page 292).

I've included some other variations of baked creams in this section, such as pear crème caramel and rice pudding, but you will find my coffee bread and butter pudding on page 291. As with other types of baked cream puddings, you can add a wide variety of flavourings to bread and butter pudding

PEAR CRÈME CARAMEL ⓖⓕ

A baked custard is transformed by the simple addition of caramel. You can flavour the custard with vanilla, cinnamon or other spices, but my favourite is this version, which I first wrote for my book *Citrus and Spice* (2008).

SERVES 6

3 ripe pears, peeled, cored and roughly chopped
55ml/2fl oz full-fat milk
200ml/7fl oz double cream
1 vanilla pod, split
3 medium eggs

3 medium egg yolks
100g/3½ oz caster sugar
150g/5½ oz granulated sugar
150ml/5fl oz boiling water

1 Put the pears in a saucepan with 1 tablespoon water. Cover and set over a medium-low heat. Simmer for 15 minutes or until the pears are meltingly soft. Purée and measure out 250ml/9fl oz of the purée.

2 Meanwhile, put the milk, cream and vanilla pod in a saucepan over a medium-low heat. Bring to just below boiling point, remove from the heat, cover and leave to infuse for 20 minutes. Remove the vanilla pod.

3 Put the eggs and egg yolks in a large bowl with the caster sugar. Whisk lightly and mix in the vanilla-infused milk and the measured 250ml/9fl oz pear purée. Strain the mixture into a jug, cover and chill for 2 hours, giving it the occasional stir if the mixture separates slightly. It will thicken as it cools.

4 Preheat the oven to fan 140°C/gas 2. Put the granulated sugar in a heavy-bottomed saucepan with the boiling water. Set over a low heat and stir occasionally until the sugar has dissolved. Bring up to the boil, and boil until it is a rich golden caramel colour, then pour into six 150ml/5fl oz ramekin dishes. Work quickly as the caramel will continue to darken as you pour.

5 Arrange the ramekins in a roasting pan. Skim any froth from the custard and pour into the ramekins. Add enough cold water to the roasting pan to come two-thirds up the sides of the ramekins. Bake for 40–50 minutes or until set, with a faint wobble. Remove from the water and chill for at least 6 hours.

6 To serve, loosen the edges of each custard with a knife, then place a rimmed plate over the top of each ramekin and invert it so that the custard slips out with its caramel sauce.

ELIZABETH RAFFALD'S ORANGE CUSTARDS

Mrs Raffald is of the great heroines of English cooking. Her simple, clear recipes were an instant hit when they were first published in *The Experienced English Housekeeper* in 1769. She influenced many cookery writers, from her near-contemporaries Hannah Glasse and Mrs Rundell, to Elizabeth David and Jane Grigson in the twentieth century.

In the eighteenth century, sour Seville oranges would have been used for this recipe. Today, their sale is restricted to the last three weeks of January, so this is a very seasonal dish. Mrs Raffald recommended this dish as 'a pretty corner-dish for dinner or side-dish for supper'. It has a wonderful delicate orange flavour and creamy texture.

SERVES 6

1 Seville orange
1 tablespoon brandy
4 medium egg yolks, strained

115g/4oz caster sugar
285ml/10fl oz double cream
285ml/10fl oz single cream

1 Preheat the oven to fan 130°C/gas 1. Line a deep roasting pan with a few sheets of kitchen paper. Place six 150ml/5fl oz ovenproof china pots in the pan.

2 Using a potato peeler, finely pare the zest of the Seville orange. Place in a small pan and cover with plenty of cold water. Bring to the boil and bubble vigorously for 5 minutes, then drain.

3 Squeeze the juice from the orange. Pour into a food processor, discarding any pips. Add half the blanched orange zest, the brandy, egg yolks and sugar. Whiz until the orange zest is finely chopped. Scrape the mixture into a large jug.

4 Pour the double and single cream into a small pan and scald by bringing to just below boiling point over a high heat. Do not let the cream boil. Slowly pour a thin stream of hot cream into the egg yolk mixture, stirring all the time. Skim off any froth and pour into the china pots.

5 Pour enough just-boiled water into the roasting pan to come halfway up the sides of the pots. Place in the oven and bake for 30 minutes, then increase the temperature to fan 140°C/gas 2 and cook for a further 30 minutes or until just set. The custards will still wobble in the middle. Cool slightly before chilling in the fridge. Once chilled, they will set to a creamy custard.

6 Cut the remaining blanched orange zest into fine shreds and keep covered in the fridge. To serve, garnish each pot with the orange zest.

ALMOND RICE PUDDING

This pudding is unusual in that it is made with basmati rice, which, once cooked, has a fluffier, drier texture than a traditional short-grain pudding rice.

For the best results, buy whole almonds in their skins and blanch them by soaking the kernels in boiling water for 5 minutes and then slipping off their brown skins. They have a stronger almond flavour than bought blanched almonds.

SERVES 6

15g/½ oz butter, plus extra for greasing
750ml/26fl oz full-fat milk
115g/4oz granulated sugar
1 teaspoon ground cinnamon

85g/3oz whole blanched almonds
225g/8oz basmati rice
55g/2oz sultanas

1 Preheat the oven to fan 140°C/gas 2. Liberally butter a deep 1.8kg/4lb pie dish. Using a small, serrated knife, cut the almonds into strips.

2 Place the milk, sugar, cinnamon and almonds in a saucepan and set over a low heat. Stir occasionally until the sugar has dissolved, then scald by bringing to just below boiling point. Remove from the heat.

3 Melt 15g/½ oz butter in a large saucepan over a medium heat. Add the rice and stir regularly for about 3 minutes or until the grains look translucent. Add the sultanas and almond milk. Bring to the boil, stir and tip into the buttered dish. Cover the dish with foil and bake for 1 hour. Remove and serve warm.

COCONUT RICE PUDDING (GF)

This pudding has a surprisingly light texture. You need deep dishes as the liquid rises up as it cooks, although it deflates as it cools.

SERVES 4

butter for greasing
4 tablespoons light muscovado sugar
3 tablespoons desiccated coconut
55g/2oz short-grain (pudding) rice

pinch of salt
3 tablespoons dark rum
85ml/3fl oz double cream
465ml/16½ fl oz full-fat milk

1 Preheat the oven to fan 140°C/gas 2. Liberally butter four 170ml/6fl oz deep soufflé dishes.

2 Put the sugar, coconut, rice, salt, rum, cream and milk into a saucepan over a medium heat. Bring to the boil, then simmer gently for 20 minutes, stirring regularly.

3 Divide the rice and liquid evenly between the buttered soufflé dishes. Place in a roasting pan (to catch any drips). Bake for 30 minutes, or until the rice is meltingly tender and the liquid has been absorbed. It should form a golden skin. Leave to rest for 10 minutes before serving. It's equally good eaten warm or cold.

THE
MILL

THE MILL

One of the defining factors of British taste is simplicity. Our cooking is characterised by our fondness for pure flavours and few ingredients. Nowhere is this more important than in baking. Source superlative flours and your bread will taste amazing. Add a fine butter and a little salt to your scone flour and you'll have a delicious teatime treat the envy of the world.

Prior to industrialisation, the landscape was dotted with windmills and watermills, all grinding locally grown grain for local markets. The countryside was a patchwork of small fields growing wheat, barley, oats and rye. Where the soil was poor or the weather cold and damp, barley, rye and oats were dominant. Wheat only predominated in the drier counties, particularly those that had access to rich markets such as London. Farmers often hedged their bets by planting wheat and rye together. If the weather was fine, the wheat would flourish, if cold and damp, the rye would harvest well. Millers mixed and matched their grain to produce everything from the finest white wheat flour to maslin flour, an often coarse blend of barley, rye and wheat.

It's hard to appreciate today, but flour once varied enormously in taste, texture and quality, depending on where you bought it. In the eighteenth century, cookery books often gave instructions to sift and dry flour before using in a fine pastry. Industrialisation

has brought many benefits to British cooks, but in its search for uniformity and reliability, much of the character of certain foods, such as flour and butter, has been lost.

If you were to step into a modern grain store while the harvest is under way, you would be amazed by the intense sweet smell of the newly threshed wheat as it pours out of a combine harvester. It's wonderful. Stand inside a working watermill, such as Winchester City Mill in Hampshire, and, amidst the mechanical whirring and flour dust, you can almost taste the toasty sweet notes of the Solstice hard wheat as it is ground between the huge millstones. This is the true flavour of wheat flour. Transformed into bread, pastry and biscuits, artisan flours can make simple recipes taste utterly delicious.

The flavour of flour varies according to the varieties of wheat used, the soil and the weather. Enthusiastic cooks should seek out artisan flours and experiment. By gaining a greater understanding of different flours, you can improve your food by simply altering a single ingredient. A fragrant Maris Widgeon wheat makes gorgeous pastry quite unlike that made from industrially milled flour, and the addition of some medium-ground oatmeal to plain flour makes scrumptious scones.

ABOVE LEFT Pitstone Windmill, Buckinghamshire, is one of the oldest post mills in England.

ABOVE RIGHT Sacks of grain waiting to be ground into flour at Houghton Mill, Cambridgeshire.

The current renaissance in bread-making has led many supermarkets to offer a wider choice of flour than ten years ago. Nevertheless, if we want to transform our baking, local mills need greater support. Artisan millers often work in collaboration with local farmers who grow traditional or unusual varieties of grains. A closer relationship between local farmers and consumers could lead to a greater revival in older grain varieties. Most grow more slowly than modern hybrids, but need less fertiliser and are more resistant to problems such as drought and pests. Their yield is lower, hence their fall from favour, but if they were ultimately more sustainable and had a ready local market, who knows how the rural landscape might change.

ABOVE LEFT Fountains Mill is a twelfth-century cornmill on the Fountains Abbey Estate, Yorkshire.

ABOVE RIGHT Eighteenth-century machinery at Houghton Mill, Cambridgeshire.

UNDERSTANDING GRAINS

WHEAT

Every country child is familiar with fields of wheat, rippling in the breeze. Many will have nibbled the sweet grains as they ripen in the summer heat, but few will relate that delicious nutty flavour to the dusty bag of flour in the kitchen. Yet flour, especially wheat flour, is a magical ingredient.

The first step towards transforming your base ingredient of flour into something exquisite is to understand it. Wheat is often called 'hard' or 'strong', or 'weak' or 'soft'. This refers to the ease with which the grains can be milled. Hard wheat has a relatively high protein level, which also means that it has a high gluten level. Gluten allows wet dough to stretch and capture air bubbles if kneaded. The majority of English-grown wheat varieties are types of soft wheat. They still contain gluten, but a type that breaks more easily. Used unblended, they will produce a more 'holey' bread like the Italian ciabatta.

As a result, many of our bread flours are a mixture of hard Canadian wheat and softer English varieties. If a farmer is supplying a small mill, however, he may grow a harder wheat variety such as Solstice that is suitable for bread. English wheat flour is perfect for cakes, biscuits, pastry and Italian-style bread.

Look out for heritage flours. These are made from old English wheat varieties, which are starting to be grown again in our fields. They produce a lovely flavoured flour.

STONEGROUND FLOUR

The traditional way to grind flour is between two stones. The resulting flour then has to be sifted to make plain white flour. Industrially produced flour is usually rolled through steel cylinders which are designed to siphon off the different elements to produce everything from bran to superfine white flour for cake-baking. Fresh stoneground flour should have a wonderful smell and delicate taste.

WHOLEMEAL FLOUR

Wholemeal flour is made by grinding the de-husked whole wheat grain, in other words it contains the ground bran, germ and starchy endosperm. This is the most nutritious type of flour, but it produces dense-textured, heavy breads and pastries – hence wholemeal flour's reputation for being 'worthy'. Luckily, that doesn't mean it can't also be delicious.

BROWN FLOUR

This is a variation of wholemeal. It contains slightly less of the entire wheat grain than wholemeal.

MALTED GRAIN FLOUR

Bread-making enthusiasts often have a bag of malted flour in their cupboard. Usually malted flakes of wheat, rye and/or barley (see barley, opposite) are mixed into wholemeal flour, although depending on the whim of the miller, malted grain flour might also contain malt or rye flour. Every mill creates their own variations, including light and dark malted flours. It's worth experimenting with different brands to find which one you like the best.

STRONG FLOUR OR BREAD FLOUR

Strong flour (made from hard wheat) has a higher protein content than soft wheat flour, and makes good bread. It may be sold as wholemeal, stoneground or white. If you enjoy making bread, it is worth trying different sources to find a really flavoursome strong flour. Many mills have a mail-order service.

PLAIN FLOUR

Sometimes called all-purpose flour, plain flour is a fine-textured white flour that has been milled from the endosperm of wheat grain. It has a higher starch content and lower protein content than strong flour, but can be used for everything, including bread or pizza, if you have no strong flour to hand.

SUPERFINE FLOUR

This is what it says on the label, an ultra-fine milled flour that some cake-makers like to use as it is said to create very light cakes. It may also be sold as cake flour.

SELF-RAISING FLOUR

This is plain white or wholemeal flour that has had a raising agent – some form of baking powder – added to it. This saves time, but you have to watch the use-by date because, once mixed into the flour, the raising agent has a relatively short shelf life. If you don't often bake cakes or puddings that need self-raising flour, it is more cost-effective to add baking powder to plain flour when needed. Use a maximum of 4 teaspoons baking powder per 250g/9oz plain flour and mix thoroughly. Keep an eye on the use-by date of your baking powder. For further information on raising agents, see page 96.

BARLEY

Barley has a short growing season and a hardy nature that makes it perfectly suited for the British Isles, particularly where the soil is poor such as in the northern uplands of England. It's a nutritious grain and comes in two forms for baking: barley flour and malted grains. Both add a nutty, sweet flavour to dishes. Barley flour is ground pearl barley.

Malted barley grains are germinated, then dried and lightly roasted before being mixed into a wheat flour with other types of malted grain. Malted barley is particularly sweet-tasting because the malting process modifies starches into sugars. Barley grains absorb twice as much water as wheat. Barley flour has a different texture to wheat flour, so to retain a good texture, use up to 30 per cent of barley flour with 70 per cent wheat flour. Barley is unsuitable for coeliacs (who cannot tolerate gluten). It contains gluten, but in a different form from wheat.

RYE

Once widely grown in Britain, rye is now mainly imported. It is primarily used in bread and crispbreads. It behaves differently to wheat flour and produces a much heavier dough that is less elastic and gas-retentive. You have to add far more water to a rye dough, otherwise it will bake into a rock-hard loaf. It also needs acidity to improve its flavour and to counteract the fact that its weak gluten structure naturally collapses during baking.

Most bakers use a sourdough starter for rye bread to maximise its flavour, but if you are in a rush, you can use yoghurt or buttermilk. A small quantity of rye flour can be added to a pizza dough, but aside from bread, rye is not widely used in British baking.

Most specialist flour millers sell both dark and light rye flours. Dark is wholemeal rye flour. Light rye flour has been sifted to remove some of its bran. Chopped, cracked or kibbled rye is whole rye grains that have been crushed into two or three pieces. They're added to recipes such as pumpernickel. You can also buy malted cut rye, which is where the rye has been germinated, dried and roasted. It has an intense flavour.

Rye flour contains gluten, so is not suitable for people with coeliac disease. It remains popular with those who have wheat intolerances as it contains far less gluten than wheat.

SPELT

In recent years, nutty-tasting British-grown spelt flour has become increasingly popular. It is an ancient wheat variety that has a low gluten content and a high level of nutrients. It is not suitable for coeliacs.

Wholemeal and refined versions are sold. If you have a tendency to keep your flour for a long time, check the use-by date of spelt flour before you buy. Spelt can develop a bitter aftertaste from oxidation if it has been stored too long.

Spelt can be treated like ordinary wheat flour, but it has a slightly weaker gluten than strong flour, and as a result it produces a shorter-textured, denser bread. Refined spelt can be used in shortbread, biscuits, scones and crumbles.

OATS

Although in the English psyche oats are primarily a Scottish food, the vast majority eaten in Britain are grown in England, in the warm damp climes of the south-west and West Midlands.

Oats have to be dried out in a kiln before the miller lightly grinds them to remove their outer casing and reveal the 'groat', which has a sweet, nutty flavour. The groat can be ground into six different grades of oatmeal. Three choices are usually available to domestic cooks: coarse, medium and fine. Medium and fine oatmeal can be used in oat cakes, soda bread and scones. Coarse oatmeal can also be used for some breads.

Rolled oats (oatflakes or porridge oats) are made from pinhead oatmeal – the roughest cut of groat. These are steamed, rolled and dried, which allows them to cook quickly. Some of their flavour and nutrients are lost in the process. Rolled oats are good in flapjacks and sprinkled over rolls before baking. Oats have a low gluten content. Store them in a cool, dark place as oats have a high oil content.

GLUTEN-FREE FLOUR

Gluten-free flour is usually made up of a mixture of different gluten-free starches such as maize, potato and tapioca flours. Since gluten-free flour does not act like a wheat flour, you should think of it as a separate product. It can make biscuits and pastry and, unlike normal flour, it does not need to be rested or mind how much you roll it. It can be substituted for wheat flour where only a little flour is required, but you may have to adapt the recipe slightly as it tends to absorb more liquid. Gluten-free flour cannot naturally form airy bubbles, so only use specialist recipes for cakes. Although I've included a few gluten-free recipes in this book, it is best to turn to a specialist cookery book for in-depth information.

PASTRY

If there is one food that will tempt the average English man or woman, it's a pastry. Pie or tart, it doesn't matter, there is something utterly seductive about the crumbling texture of homemade pastry melting in your mouth with an unctuous filling.

This deep-seated love stretches back to at least the mid-sixteenth century. Since then, English cooks have developed dozens of different pastry recipes. Pastry could be made with cream or a hot mixture of ale and melted butter, or even beef or mutton broth with melted butter. The pastry dough could be enriched with egg yolks or coloured yellow with saffron. The type of flour varied from fine white wheat flour for the rich to barley meal for the servants.

Strange, then, that as a nation we appear to have developed a phobia about making pastry. You just have to mention homemade pastry and someone will groan and say ruefully, 'Oh, I can't make pastry.' Even more bizarre is the fact that many cookery writers now advocate buying ready-made pastry rather than addressing the problem. Many chefs admit to buying frozen puff pastry rather than making it themselves.

Contrary to such teachings, I would urge everyone to try their hand at making pastry. It's fun, easy and tastes absolutely wonderful, far better than bought – even when it goes wrong! Believe me, I know. I spent years worrying about making pastry, convinced that it took cool hands, marble work tops and the lightest of touches. All I had was a mixing bowl, a wobbly old fridge as a work surface and the wrong sort of rolling pin that my flat-mate had accidentally burnt on the gas cooker.

I still use my old rolling pin and realise now, with the benefit of experience, that the key to making good pastry is confidence. Remember, it doesn't matter if the pastry shrinks slightly

because you've added too much water or is very crumbly because you haven't added enough water, it's still going to taste yummy. Of course, you should be sensitive in how you approach your ingredients, but it really isn't difficult to make pastry. And the more you make it, the easier it becomes.

The main problem for most cooks today is allowing sufficient time for the pastry to chill. If you're making textbook pastry, you should chill it in the fridge for 30 minutes after mixing the dough together, and then for another 30 minutes after rolling. I was taught that this was to allow the stretchy gluten in the dough to relax, so that the pastry wouldn't be tough. However, I think that the main benefit is that the fat is sufficiently chilled to ensure that the pastry holds its shape as it cooks. I cheat and skip a chilling by rolling my shortcrust pastry straight after I've made the dough and then I rest it for 30 minutes. I don't think that it makes much difference and it's certainly much easier to roll.

Those of a nervous disposition should start by making shortcrust pastry. If you enjoy making it, move on to rough puff pastry before tackling puff pastry. This has a reputation for being harder to make because you need to let the butter cool sufficiently between each rolling so that it doesn't melt and break through the layers of dough. If this happens, the pastry is less light and flaky. I tend to make puff pastry on a day when I've got other things I need to do at home. This ensures that I'm happily occupied while the pastry is chilling in between being rolled. The final pastry can then be wrapped and frozen.

All pastry freezes well for up to a month. It's also worth freezing pastry trimmings. You can combine them by rolling together a stack of defrosted trimmings when you want to make a quick tart or pie, but remember to label which type of pastry you've frozen, as you don't want to combine puff and shortcrust trimmings.

I've included quite a few British pastry recipes in this section. You can also find a rich almond pastry, which is used for the mince pies on page 283 and a self-raising pastry on page 217 that is used for fruit pies. Although I would encourage everyone to try making pastry, don't feel bad if you choose to buy it ready-made. I buy ready-made filo pastry. When buying chilled or frozen shortcrust or puff pastry, read the ingredients label and choose the most natural-sounding – preferably made with butter as it tastes better.

Pastry: flour weight or total weight?

When pastry quantities are given in recipes, the weight of the pastry refers to the flour weight used to make the pastry, not the final weight of the pastry. This is the traditional way of expressing pastry weight, dating back to the time, not so long ago, when everyone made their own pastry. The weight of the finished pastry varies, depending on how much liquid your flour absorbs and the other ingredients used. This can cause confusion when buying ready-made pastry as the weight on the packet usually refers to the total weight of ingredients, which will be more than the flour weight.

In general, pastry made with 170g/6oz flour and 85g/3oz butter will cover a pie or tart for four people. In this book, all the pastry recipes are based on 225g/8oz flour, as this allows greater flexibility, especially for beginners rolling out their pastry. You can freeze the trimmings.

SHORTCRUST PASTRY

As with all pastry, choose a good-quality unsalted butter and ideally an organic flour to ensure a wonderful flavour. I always use half the weight of butter to flour. The quantity of water will vary with different brands of flour.

MAKES 225G/8OZ PASTRY (FLOUR WEIGHT)

225g/8oz plain flour
pinch of salt

115g/4oz chilled butter, diced
about 3 tablespoons cold water

1 Put the flour and salt in a food processor. Add the butter and process in short bursts until the mixture forms fine crumbs. Don't over-process into a paste or your pastry will be too short.

2 Tip the crumbs into a mixing bowl. Using a fork, mix in about 3 tablespoons of cold water. You want the crumbs to form themselves into larger balls of dough. If the dough is too dry, it will be crumbly when cooked. If it is too wet, it will shrink when baked and have a more brittle texture.

3 Place the dough on a scantily floured surface and lightly knead into a ball. Roll out as needed. Loosely roll the pastry around the rolling pin, lift it over the tart tin or pie, and then carefully unroll.

4 Cover and chill for 30 minutes (or longer if you like) before baking.

IF YOU WANT TO MAKE YOUR PASTRY BY HAND, SIFT THE FLOUR AND SALT INTO A LARGE MIXING BOWL. ADD THE BUTTER AND, USING YOUR FINGERTIPS, LIGHTLY RUB THE BUTTER INTO THE FLOUR UNTIL IT FORMS FINE BREADCRUMBS. THEN ADD THE COLD WATER AND CONTINUE AS ABOVE. THIS METHOD CAN BE USED TO MAKE RICH SHORTCRUST AND LARD SHORTCRUST PASTRY BY HAND (SEE PAGE 82).

RICH SHORTCRUST PASTRY

Some recipes add a little more butter to flour along with the egg, but I prefer this ratio. Some sweet recipes also add 2 tablespoons of caster sugar – after rubbing in the butter, mix in the sugar by hand before adding the egg yolk and water. I always use unsweetened pastry as it enhances the taste of the other sweet ingredients. Sugar will also make the dough brown more quickly as it's baking. If necessary, protect with foil.

If you find this richer dough difficult to roll, place it between two sheets of greaseproof paper or baking parchment and roll out to the required size.

MAKES 225G/8OZ PASTRY (FLOUR WEIGHT)

225g/8oz plain flour
pinch of salt

115g/4oz chilled butter, diced
1 medium egg yolk

1 Put the flour, salt and butter in a food processor and whiz to fine crumbs. Tip into a bowl. Beat the egg yolk with 2 tablespoons cold water. Using a fork, mix into the dough and add enough cold water to bind the dough (about a further 1–2 tablespoons).

2 Lightly knead on a floured surface, then roll out as needed. Cover and chill for 30 minutes before baking.

LARD SHORTCRUST PASTRY

In the nineteenth century, lard was a common shortening for pastry. This recipe can be used for savoury dishes or for the Yorkshire curd tart on page 54. Some recipes suggest 55g/2oz lard and 55g/2oz butter to 225g/8oz plain flour, which is also very good.

MAKES 225G/8OZ PASTRY (FLOUR WEIGHT)

225g/8oz plain flour
pinch of salt

115g/4oz cold lard, diced
1 tablespoon natural yoghurt

1 Put the flour, salt and lard in a food processor and whiz to fine crumbs. Tip into a bowl and add the yogurt and enough cold water (about 2 tablespoons) to bind the dough.

2 Lightly knead on a floured surface, then roll out as needed. Cover and chill for 30 minutes before baking.

ROUGH PUFF PASTRY

Rough puff pastry is sometimes called flaky pastry. It is a slightly quicker and less rich version of puff pastry. If you're nervous of making puff pastry, it's a good way to build up your confidence. If the butter looks as though it's melting before you've finished rolling and turning, just wrap and chill until it's firm again. Use in place of puff pastry.

MAKES 225G/8OZ PASTRY (FLOUR WEIGHT)

225g/8oz plain flour
pinch of salt
170g/6oz cold butter, diced

1 teaspoon lemon juice
120ml/4fl oz cold water

1 Sift the flour and salt into a large mixing bowl. Cut the butter into 2cm/¾ in dice and stir into the flour. Gently mix in the lemon juice and enough water to bind the flour and water into a rough dough. Turn out on to a lightly floured work surface and lightly shape into a rectangle, but do not knead.

2 Roll out the dough into a long strip about three times as long as it is wide. Mark the pastry into thirds, then fold one end up and the other down over it. Using the rolling pin, lightly press down on each edge to seal the pastry. Give the dough a half-turn clockwise.

3 Using short sharp strokes, roll out the dough so that it returns to its original length and width. Fold, turn and roll once more, then wrap in greaseproof paper and chill for 15–30 minutes. Make a note of which way the pastry is facing before chilling, as you will need to continue with the clockwise half-turns.

4 After resting the pastry, replace on the floured surface in the position that you left off and continue with a further two rolls and half-turns. Chill for another 30 minutes, and then make two more rolls and half-turns. Wrap and chill until needed or cut in half and freeze.

PUFF PASTRY

In 1609, in his still-practical book *Delightes for Ladies*, Sir Hugh Plat describes how 'To make puffe paste'. He mixes whole eggs and extra egg white into the finest flour, before placing 'small peeces of butter as big as Nuts upon it, then folde it over, then drive it abroade againe, then put small peeces of butter upon it as did before, doe this tenne times, always folding the paste and putting butter betweene everie folde'. In comparison, modern English puff pastry seems very simple.

The pastry itself doesn't take long to make, but it needs to be rested regularly in between rollings. The chilling times are the minimum period of time you should leave the dough, but you can leave it several hours if you like. Incidentally, should you feel inspired, Sir Hugh Plat recommends cherry tart, rice or pippins be served between two sheets of puff pastry.

MAKES 225G/8OZ PASTRY (FLOUR WEIGHT)

225g/8oz plain flour
pinch of salt

225g/8oz cold butter
120ml/4fl oz cold water

1 Mix together the flour and salt in a food processor. Add 30g/1oz diced cold butter and whiz until it forms fine crumbs. Tip into a bowl and mix in about 120ml/4fl oz cold water or enough to form a rough dough. Lightly knead into a ball and wrap in a polythene bag. Chill for 30 minutes.

2 Fifteen minutes before you are ready to roll, take the remaining 200g/7oz butter out of the fridge and let it soften slightly. Place the butter between two sheets of clingfilm and use a rolling pin to flatten it into a 2.5cm/1in thick rectangle.

3 On a floured surface, roll out the dough into a rectangle that is three times the length of the butter and about 2.5cm/1in wider than the butter. Place the butter in the centre of the dough and then fold over the top and bottom flaps of dough, so that the butter is completely covered. Using the rolling pin, lightly press down on each edge so that the butter is sealed in. Give the dough a half-turn clockwise.

4 Using short sharp strokes, roll out the dough so that it returns to its original length (three times that of the butter) but retains the same thickness. Then fold in the top and bottom ends, press the edges with the rolling pin and give a further half-turn clockwise. If the butter is breaking through the pastry or the pastry is becoming warm, stop, wrap and chill for 30 minutes. If not, you can repeat the rolling process one more time before resting the dough. Make a note of which way the dough is facing before chilling, as you will need to continue with the clockwise half-turns.

5 After 30 minutes' chilling, replace the pastry on the floured surface in the position that you left off and continue with a further two rolls and half-turns. Chill for another 30 minutes and then make two more rolls and half-turns. Wrap and chill until needed or cut in half and freeze.

CHOUX PASTRY

I've included a recipe for choux pastry in this section, although it is made in a very different way from other pastries. Use it for summer berry cream puffs (see page 168) and chocolate violet éclairs (see page 305).

MAKE 24 PUFFS, 48 PROFITEROLES OR 24 SMALL ÉCLAIRS

115g/4oz plain flour
pinch of salt
115g/4oz butter, diced

300ml/10½ fl oz water
4 small eggs, beaten

1 Preheat the oven to fan 200°C/gas 7. Oil a non-stick baking sheet. Sift the salt and flour into a bowl.

2 Put the butter and water in a small saucepan. Bring to a brisk boil and, as soon as the butter has melted, take off the heat and tip in the flour. Beat vigorously with a wooden spoon for 3–4 minutes over a low heat until the mixture is smooth and glossy and leaves the side of the saucepan.

3 Remove from the heat and beat in the eggs, a little at a time. Stop beating once the dough is smooth and glossy but stiff enough to hold its shape.

Cream puffs – if you're making cream puffs, use two teaspoons to spoon out 24 blobs on to the baking sheet, spacing them well apart. Bake for 25 minutes or until dry and crisp. Using a skewer, quickly pierce each puff and return to the switched-off oven for 5 minutes, leaving the door slightly open. This allows any steam to escape. Cool on a wire rack.

Profiteroles – if you're making profiteroles, spoon or pipe out small teaspoon-sized blobs on to the baking sheet, spacing them well apart. Bake for 15 minutes or until dry and crisp. Using a skewer, pierce each profiterole and return to the switched-off oven for 5 minutes, leaving the door slightly open. Cool on a wire rack.

Éclairs – if you're making small éclairs, spoon the pastry into a piping bag with a 1cm/½ in nozzle. Pipe 9cm/ 3½ in lengths of pastry on to the baking sheet. Bake for 12 minutes or until golden. Using a small knife, make a slit along the side of each éclair. Return to the oven, turn off the heat, and leave the door slightly open for 5 minutes to dry out the pastry. Cool on a wire rack.

NECTARINE SLICE

Peaches and nectarines were once commonly grown in England on south- and south-east-facing walls. John Worlidge, in his *Systema Agriculturae* of 1697, advises that both should be grown on walls or in glasshouses. The Egerton family at Tatton Park in Cheshire, for example, were supplied with peaches and nectarines from their extensive glass houses in the eighteenth century.

This is a simple, modern pastry which works well with buttery homemade puff pastry. You can adapt this recipe to use other fruit such as apples, pears and plums.

My homemade puff pastry, made from 225g/8oz flour, weighed about 565g/1¼ lb once made: you will only need half the pastry for this dish. However, it's easier to roll out a larger piece of pastry. Carefully fold up the trimmings and freeze for another dish.

SERVES 6

225g/8oz puff pastry (see page 84)
3 ripe nectarines, quartered and stoned

1 tablespoon caster sugar or to taste
225g/8oz clotted cream, to serve

1 On a lightly floured surface, roll your pastry into a large thin rectangle about 3mm/⅛ in thick. You are only going to use half the pastry. Using a 20 x 30cm/8 x 12in Swiss roll tin as a giant pastry cutter, cut out a rectangle of that size. Take a sharp knife and lightly run it about 1cm/½ in inside the pastry edge, so that you score a line to create a rim for the tart. Prick the internal rectangle with a fork. Place on a non-stick baking sheet and chill for 30 minutes. Preheat the oven to fan 200°C/gas 7.

2 Finely slice each nectarine quarter and lay them neatly in slightly overlapping rows on the pastry, taking care not to cover the rim. Sprinkle the sugar evenly over the nectarines.

3 Bake for 20 minutes or until the pastry is crisp and the nectarines flecked gold. Serve warm or at room temperature, with clotted cream.

SAVOURY BISCUITS

Tucked away in most British kitchen cupboards is a biscuit tin. Much loved, it keeps all manner of tempting biscuits fresh. Everyone has their favourites, both sweet and savoury, although the two should never be placed in the same tin, as they can affect each other's flavours.

Throughout this book, you will find other biscuit recipes such as rosemary shortbread on page 138 and iced spiced biscuits on page 268. Some employ very different baking techniques such as the soft hazelnut macaroons on page 252 or the chocolate chip cookies on page 302. However, I thought I would begin with savoury biscuits, since they are closely related to pastry. These are often neglected in cookbooks, probably because you can buy very good-quality ready-made cheese biscuits and cheese straws. Be warned: once you've made your own, it's hard to go back to buying them.

CHEESE STRAWS

Cheese straws were the first thing that I was taught to cook at school, no doubt because everyone loves eating them. They're very easy to make and, if you don't want to make straws, you can roll out the dough and it cut into shapes such as stars and crescent moons. Perfect for drinks parties! You can also vary the topping: try poppy seeds, yellow mustard seeds or nigella seeds.

MAKES 30 CHEESE STRAWS

225g/8oz plain flour
¼ teaspoon salt
¼ teaspoon cayenne pepper
115g/4oz cold butter, diced
115g/4oz Parmesan cheese. finely grated
1 medium egg, beaten

TOPPING
½ beaten medium egg
1 heaped tablespoon caraway seeds

1 Lightly oil three baking sheets.

2 Sift the flour, salt and cayenne pepper into a large bowl. Using your fingertips, lightly rub the butter into the flour until it resembles fine breadcrumbs (or quickly whiz in the food processor then tip into a mixing bowl). Stir in the cheese, using a fork. Mix in the egg and between 2 and 5 tablespoons of cold water; this will depend on your flour. As soon as the crumbs begin to hold together, turn out on to a lightly floured surface. Lightly knead until smooth.

3 Cut the dough in half and roll out the first half to about 5mm/¼ in thick. The pastry needs to be thick enough to twist without breaking. Trim the edges and cut into strips, each about 20cm/8in long and 1cm/½ in wide. Gently twist each strip and lay on a baking sheet. Repeat with the remaining pastry. Re-roll the trimmings and repeat until you've used all the dough and made around 30 straws.

4 Carefully brush all the straws with the beaten egg and sprinkle with the caraway seeds. Chill for 30 minutes. Preheat the oven to fan 180°C/gas 5.

5 Bake the straws for 15 minutes or until golden brown. Cool on a wire rack. They will keep for a few days in an airtight tin. Serve in long glasses.

WATER BISCUITS

Water biscuits are so named because originally they were made with just flour and water. They're the descendant of ship's biscuits, a form of hard biscuit that was eaten in place of bread during long sea voyages. English versions used soft or medium-soft wheat flour, while Scottish recipes used hard (strong) wheat flour. In the early nineteenth century, the recipe developed to include fat, chemical raising agents such as bicarbonate of soda and sometimes sweetening.

Homemade water biscuits are best eaten on the day of baking. They may become soft if stored in an airtight container. To make them crisp again, place in a preheated oven (fan 170°C/gas 4) for a few minutes. Cool before serving. Compared to the crisp wafer-thin shop-bought biscuits, these are more crumbly. They're very addictive.

MAKES ABOUT 30 BISCUITS

225g/8oz plain white flour, sifted
1 teaspoon baking powder
½ teaspoon salt, plus extra sea salt for sprinkling

55g/2oz cold lard, diced
100ml/3½ fl oz very cold water

1 Preheat the oven to fan 170°C/gas 4. Lightly grease three non-stick baking sheets. Sift the flour, baking powder and ½ teaspoon salt into a food processor and mix thoroughly. Add the lard and process until the mixture forms tiny crumbs. Tip into a mixing bowl.

2 Add the water and mix into a firm dough. You may need to add another tablespoon of cold water, depending on your flour. Turn out on to a floured surface. Lightly knead, cut in half and roll out into a very thin sheet, as thin as you can go without the dough breaking. Stamp out using a 7cm/2¾ in diameter pastry cutter. Using a palette knife, gently transfer to the baking sheets and sprinkle with sea salt. Repeat with the remaining dough. Knead together the trimmings and repeat until you've used all the dough.

3 Bake for 15 minutes or until pale golden. Cool on a wire rack. Serve or store once cold.

OAT CAKES

Oat cakes only take a few minutes to make and keep very well in an airtight tin. Delicious with cheese, they're also useful for packed lunches – or try them with a homemade smoked trout or salmon pâté.

MAKES ABOUT 18 BISCUITS

225g/8oz medium oatmeal
2 tablespoons plain flour
¼ teaspoon fine sea salt

½ teaspoon bicarbonate of soda
½ tablespoon melted butter
about 100ml/3½ fl oz warm water

1 Preheat the oven to fan 190°C/gas 6. Lightly grease two non-stick baking sheets.

2 Mix together the oatmeal, 2 tablespoons flour, salt and bicarbonate of soda in a bowl. Stir in the melted butter and about 100ml/3½ fl oz warm water or enough to form a firm dough. Turn out and lightly knead for 2 minutes or until smooth. If the dough breaks up, it needs a little more water. Don't worry, just stick it back in the bowl, knead in more water, and try again.

3 On a lightly floured work surface, roll out the dough until it is about 3mm/⅛ in thick, then cut out small discs or triangles. Place on two non-stick baking sheets. Knead together the trimmings, adding more water if necessary, re-roll, and cut out more oat cakes until you have used up all the dough.

4 Bake for 8–10 minutes or until lightly coloured and crisp. Cool on a wire rack. Serve cold.

SCONES &
SODA BREADS

Scones were originally cooked on a griddle – a flat iron plate heated over a flame – like a thick pancake, but as domestic ovens became widespread in the latter part of the nineteenth century, cooks started to bake them in an oven. At the same time, commercially produced chemical raising agents such as bicarbonate of soda and baking powder became widely available. Suddenly scones and soda breads could be made at a moment's notice.

There are two main methods of making scones: with and without eggs. The latter are a form of soda bread. The key to making plump, fluffy scones is to make a soft dough that is handled lightly and quickly, before rolling out to no less than 2cm/¾ in thick. The thickness ensures that they rise properly. If you apply more pressure with your rolling pin on parts of the dough, the scone will list slightly to one side.

Soda breads are very similar. For the best results make sure that the dough is soft, and handled quickly and lightly, before placing in a hot oven.

Raising agents

Bicarbonate of soda, or baking soda as it is known in America, is alkaline and produces carbon dioxide as soon as it is mixed with an acidic ingredient such as buttermilk, soured cream or yoghurt. The carbon dioxide forms little bubbles in the batter or dough, which expand when subjected to heat and become trapped in the cake or bread. Since the reaction starts immediately, it's important to get the batter or dough into the oven quickly, so you shouldn't knead soda bread or leave a gingerbread batter waiting. Incidentally, bicarbonate of soda gives white flour a slightly yellowish tinge when cooked.

Modern baking powder was invented in 1843 by Alfred Bird of Bird's Custard Powder fame. According to Nicholas Kurti's entertaining

essay in *But the Crackling is Superb* (1988), Mr Bird was a young pharmaceutical chemist whose wife, Elizabeth Lavinia Ragg, suffered from a digestive disorder that prevented her from eating anything prepared with eggs or with yeast. Like any sensible woman, she craved custard to accompany her favourite fruit pies, so the brilliant young Alfred developed an eggless custard powder for her pleasure, which in turn made their fortune. No doubt in response to her desire for bread, he invented baking powder. It was manufactured by his company and was used by the British Army to make fresh bread during the Crimean War.

In essence, baking powder utilises the raising process of bicarbonate of soda by combining alkaline bicarbonate of soda with an acid in the form of tiny solid crystals such as cream of tartar (tartaric acid). Baking powder also contains a filler to keep the mixture dry, which is now usually a gluten-free flour such as rice flour. Check the ingredients list if you have a gluten allergy. Once liquid is added, the baking powder starts to work and the same rules apply as with bicarbonate of soda.

Since baking powder has a relatively short shelf life, always check its use-by date. If it's passed, you can always mix your own for immediate use. To raise 450g/1lb flour, use 4 level teaspoons of cream of tartar to 2 teaspoons of bicarbonate of soda.

Both baking powder and bicarbonate of soda can make scones or cakes look speckled if they're not mixed into the flour properly. It's important to stick to the exact measurements. Don't heap teaspoons, as too much of either will leave a bitter aftertaste.

TRADITIONAL SWEET SCONES

Scones have become an essential element of a British afternoon tea. The National Trust has created many variations of its classic recipe (see below) for its restaurants and cafés, many of which have links to historic recipes or family favourites. If you like a glossy crust on your scones, paint the tops with beaten egg before baking. For a lighter gloss and softer scone, brush with milk instead, or just dust with flour before baking.

MAKES 8 SCONES

225g/8oz self-raising flour
½ teaspoon salt
55g/2oz cold butter, diced

30g/1oz caster sugar
150ml/5fl oz full-fat milk

1 Preheat the oven to fan 200°C/gas 7. Lightly oil a non-stick baking sheet.

2 Sift the flour and salt into a food processor. Add the butter, whiz to fine crumbs, and then tip the mixture into a bowl. Otherwise, sift the flour and salt into a bowl and, using your fingertips, rub the butter into the flour until it resembles fine breadcrumbs.

3 Stir in the sugar, then add the milk and mix until it forms a soft dough. Turn out on to a lightly floured surface and lightly knead the dough until it is just smooth. The raising agent starts to work as soon as the liquid is added, so it's essential to be quick at this stage.

4 Roll out the dough evenly to about 2.5cm/1in thick. Dust a 7cm/2¾ in diameter pastry cutter in flour and quickly stamp out your scones. Place on the baking sheet. Gather the scraps together, re-roll and cut out more scones.

5 Bake for 20 minutes or until well risen and brown.

NATIONAL TRUST SCONE VARIATIONS

Fruit scones Add 115g/4oz raisins with the sugar.

Apricot scones Add 115g/4oz chopped dried apricots with the sugar.

Treacle scones Add an extra 30g/1oz self-raising flour; warm the milk, and add 60g/2¼ oz black treacle to the warm milk.

Rose scones Add ½ teaspoon distilled rose water to the milk.

Strawberry scones Add 70g/2½ oz chopped fresh strawberries with 10ml (2 teaspoons) less milk.

Raspberry scones Add 70g/2½ oz gently crushed raspberries with 10ml (2 teaspoons) less milk.

Cheese scones Add 115g/4oz grated hard cheese, a pinch of English mustard powder and a pinch of cayenne pepper after the butter has been rubbed in. Omit the sugar.

Blue cheese scones Add 115g/4oz finely crumbled blue cheese after the butter has been rubbed in. Omit the sugar.

OAT SCONES

These are hearty scones that will keep out the cold on a winter day. They make a lovely breakfast: bake ahead and freeze, then defrost in the oven and serve warm with lots of butter. They taste particularly good with elderberry jelly (see page 243).

MAKES 12 SCONES

115g/4oz plain white flour
55g/2oz stoneground wholemeal flour, plus extra
    for dusting
55g/2oz medium oatmeal

½ teaspoon salt
½ teaspoon bicarbonate of soda
100ml/3½ fl oz buttermilk or natural yoghurt
about 100ml/3½ fl oz cold water

1 Preheat the oven to fan 200°C/gas 7. Lightly oil a non-stick baking sheet.

2 Put all the dry ingredients in a large bowl and mix thoroughly. Mix in the buttermilk or yoghurt, followed by enough water to form a soft dough. Don't worry if it's a bit sticky, or even very sticky, just plop it down on a liberally wholemeal-floured surface. Quickly shape into a round and dust in flour on both sides.

3 Liberally dust your rolling pin with flour and roll out the dough to 2.5cm/1in thick. Using a floured 6cm/2½ in diameter fluted pastry cutter, firmly stamp out the scones. Place on the baking sheet. Lightly squash the trimmings together and re-roll until you've used all the dough.

4 Bake for 20 minutes or until lightly coloured, risen and cooked through. They won't rise as much as ordinary scones. Serve hot, warm or at room temperature.

OLIVE AND ONION SCONES

This is an example of a savoury scone made with egg. You can alter the flavourings, for example, by adding diced ham instead of olives. These are particularly good served with soup or cheese.

MAKES 8 SCONES

2 tablespoons extra virgin olive oil
1 onion, finely diced
8 green olives, diced
225g/8oz self-raising flour, plus extra for dusting

pinch of salt
55g/2oz cold butter, diced
1 medium egg, beaten
about 90ml/3¼ fl oz full-fat milk

1 Preheat the oven to fan 200°C/gas 7. Lightly oil a non-stick baking sheet.

2 Place a small frying pan over a medium heat. Add the olive oil and gently fry the onion for 10 minutes or until soft and golden. Tip into a small bowl and mix in the diced olives.

3 Sift the flour and salt into a food processor. Add the butter, whiz to fine crumbs, and then tip the crumbs into a bowl. Otherwise, sift the flour and salt into a mixing bowl and, using your fingertips, rub the butter into the flour until it resembles fine breadcrumbs.

4 Beat the egg in a measuring jug and add enough milk to measure just under 150ml/5fl oz. Mix the onion and olives into the flour mixture and stir in the egg mixture until it forms a soft dough. Turn out on to a lightly floured surface and lightly knead the dough until it is just smooth.

5 Roll out the dough evenly to about 2.5cm/1in thick. Dust a 7cm/2¾ in diameter pastry cutter in flour and quickly stamp out your scones. Place on the baking sheet. Gather the scraps together, re-roll and cut out more scones.

6 Bake for 20 minutes or until well risen and brown. Cool on a wire rack. You can freeze the scones for up to 1 month.

DATE AND WALNUT TEA-BREAD

Tea-breads can be eaten as a cake or as a sweet-fruited bread, spread with butter. They're very easy to make and freeze well. Tea-breads use the 'melting' method of cake-making. This is an eggless cake and depends on its raising agents to rise.

You can play with this recipe by adding spices, changing the fruit and nuts, the type of flour or the type of sugar, provided you stick to the proportions given here.

MAKES A 450G/1LB LOAF

270ml/9½ fl oz full-fat milk
85g/3oz black treacle
55g/2oz butter
finely grated zest of 1 orange
340g/12oz stoneground wholemeal flour
1 tablespoon baking powder

½ teaspoon salt
½ teaspoon bicarbonate of soda
85g/3oz dark muscovado sugar
85g/3oz raisins
115g/4oz stoned dates, roughly chopped
55g/2oz walnuts, roughly chopped

1 Preheat the oven to fan 170°C/gas 4. Grease a 900g/2lb loaf tin, line the base and ends with a strip of baking parchment, and lightly grease.

2 Put the milk, black treacle, butter and orange zest into a small saucepan. Set over a low heat and stir occasionally until the butter has melted. Leave to cool.

3 Sift the flour, baking powder, salt and bicarbonate of soda into a mixing bowl. Mix thoroughly. Stir in the sugar, raisins, dates and walnuts. Stir the cooled milk mixture into the flour and mix thoroughly until you have a smooth batter. Scrape into the loaf tin and bake for 45–50 minutes or until well risen and golden. Test by inserting a skewer into the centre of the cake: if it comes out clean, the cake is cooked. Transfer to a wire rack and leave until tepid. Then turn out of its tin.

COTEHELE MILL SODA BREAD

Step into the National Trust's Cotehele watermill and, amidst the splashing sound of the water and the massive creakings of the woodwork turning the grinding millstones, you will be struck by the wonderful smell of freshly ground, locally grown wheat. Their simple recipe for soda bread is the quickest way to appreciate such flour. Ideally, it should be eaten on the day it's made, preferably warm with lots of unsalted butter, but it still tastes good the next day.

MAKES A 450G/1LB LOAF

450g/1lb stoneground wholemeal flour
1 teaspoon bicarbonate of soda
1½ teaspoons salt

150ml/5fl oz soured cream
150ml/5fl oz water

1 Preheat the oven to fan 200°C/gas 7. Lightly grease a baking sheet or line with baking parchment.

2 Mix the flour, bicarbonate of soda and salt in a bowl. Whisk together the cream and water. Stir the thinned cream into the flour. Mix together and, if necessary, add a little more water until you have a soft but not sticky dough.

3 Turn out on to a clean, lightly floured surface and quickly shape into a soft, fairly smooth, round loaf. Place on the baking sheet and cut a deep cross in the top of the loaf.

4 Bake for 30 minutes. Keep an eye on it towards the last 5–10 minutes and cover with foil for the last 5 minutes if it is going too brown. It is cooked when it sounds hollow if tapped on its bottom.

5 Leave to cool on a wire rack for at least 15 minutes before eating. If you want a softer crust, wrap in a tea towel as it cools.

BACON SODA BREAD

Like all soda breads, this is best eaten on the day it's made. However, if you want to serve it for breakfast, you can prepare the ingredients the night before and mix them together in the morning. Cover and chill the fried bacon. Mix, cover and chill the water and soured cream. This bread is particularly good served with tomato soup.

MAKES A 450G/1LB LOAF

2 tablespoons cold-pressed rapeseed oil
150g/5½ oz (6 slices) dry-cured back bacon (smoked or unsmoked), trimmed of fat and finely diced
450g/1lb plain white flour

1 teaspoon bicarbonate of soda
1½ teaspoons salt
150ml/5fl oz soured cream
150ml/5fl oz water

1 Preheat the oven to fan 200°C/gas 7. Lightly grease a baking sheet.

2 Set a non-stick frying pan over a medium-high heat. Add the oil, and once hot, fry the diced bacon briskly for 4–5 minutes, until lightly coloured and just beginning to turn crisp. Using a slotted spoon, remove from the pan and drain on a plate lined with kitchen paper.

3 Sift the flour, bicarbonate of soda and salt into a bowl. Mix thoroughly. Stir in the fried bacon. Whisk together the cream and water. Stir the thinned cream into the flour. Mix together and, if necessary, add a little more water until you have a soft but not sticky dough. Different flours absorb different amounts of water, so you may need to add a further 50ml/scant 2fl oz.

4 Turn out on to a clean, lightly floured surface and quickly work into a smooth dough. Shape into a round loaf, place on the baking sheet and cut a deep cross in the top of the loaf.

5 Bake for 30 minutes or until golden on top and cooked through. Keep an eye on it towards the last 5–10 minutes, and cover with foil for the last 5 minutes if it is going too brown. It is cooked when it sounds hollow if tapped on its bottom. Leave to cool on a wire rack for at least 15 minutes before eating.

BREAD

Dipping your hands into a bowl of flour and kneading silky, yeast-scented dough is one of the great pleasures in life. Choose a quiet time, slip into the kitchen and make some bread. There is something meditative about mixing, kneading, proving and baking bread. It creates an environment to think and makes you feel content with the world.

Happily, we're living in an age that is rediscovering the pleasure of bread-making. Given the space restrictions of a general baking book, I've decided not to include a recipe for sourdough bread. Instead, I'm going to give recipes for beginners, in the hope that enthusiasts will seek out specialised bread books (see bibliography, page 316) to develop their skills further. Nor am I going to give any recipes for bread-making machines, as I want to illustrate the theory behind making bread, leaving you free to choose your own bread-making path.

I've included a yeast-based pizza dough here, but you will find the recipes for rocket-topped onion olive pizza on page 149 and field mushroom calzone on page 239. There are other yeast-based recipes elsewhere in the book (see index under yeast), including a honey rum baba with pineapple on page 312.

Yeast

All you need to make a delicious loaf of bread is good flour, yeast, water and salt. For information on using different flours, see Understanding Grains on page 71. Most bread books suggest using fresh yeast, but it's not easy to find, so I would recommend using organic active dried yeast. If you can't find organic, use active dried yeast, either fast-action (the most common type) or traditional dried yeast. Fast-action yeast is also sold as easy-blend yeast. According to Andrew Whitley, in his brilliant book *Bread Matters* (2006), fast-action dried yeast comes already mixed with additives such as vitamin C and 'rehydration agent', which you mix directly into your flour. However, he explains that you get a more even dispersal of yeast, regardless of type, if you dissolve it first in tepid water (as described in each of the recipes in this

book). It also allows you to check that it is still active. The yeast is alive if it froths up and smells yeasty. This should happen within minutes; if nothing happens after 30 minutes, the yeast is dead and you need to buy a fresh supply. Contrary to popular belief, you don't need to add any sugar to the water to feed the dried yeast, although you can add a little flour if you want. If you have more than 5 per cent of sugar to the flour weight of the dough, it will inhibit the yeast activity, so extra yeast is needed.

Fast-action yeast is more concentrated than traditional active dried yeast. If you need to translate yeast quantities, I've found Andrew Whitley's metric yeast ratio very accurate: 10g fresh yeast = 5g traditional active dried yeast = 3g fast-action yeast.

Just as too much sugar can inhibit the yeast, so can too much salt, so take care not to mix the yeast and salt together initially. Salt also strengthens the gluten in the flour.

Kneading

Once you have mixed all your ingredients, it's important to knead the dough. Tip it on to a clean surface – you don't need to dust the surface with flour. To knead, use the heel of your hand to push the dough away from you, then partially fold the stretched dough back over the main part of the dough, slightly rotate the dough and repeat the process until the dough feels silky smooth and elastic.

The dough will stick a bit to start with, but it will gradually become smooth and elastic. A perfect dough is very soft rather than wet at the end of kneading, but you should always err on the side of wetness, as a stiff, firm dough will make a tough, dense-textured loaf. You can always add more water to your dough. If your hands get too gloopy, clean them by rubbing with flour and then continue.

Kneading develops the gluten structure in the dough and allows the flour to absorb more water. If you're using a machine, particularly a food processor, to mix the dough, be careful not to over-process as this can weaken the gluten – the dough will look curdled.

Proving

The next step is to leave the dough to rise or 'prove'. This allows the gluten structure in the dough to relax and become softer and more stretchy while at the same time giving the yeast time to ferment. As the yeast ferments, it releases bubbles of carbon dioxide, which are captured in the now stretchy dough; this will aerate the bread. To encourage fermentation, the dough should be placed in a large bowl and covered with clingfilm – make sure that the bowl is large enough that the dough won't touch the clingfilm once risen – and left in a place free from cold draughts. Don't rush this stage. The usual guide is that the bread should look like it's almost doubled in size. The time will vary according to the ambient temperature.

Knock back the risen dough by briefly kneading (to release some of the air) and forming into your chosen shape. If baking in a bread tin, a white dough should fill one-third of the tin and a wholemeal or fruited dough half of the tin. The dough then needs to rise once again. At this stage, there is the risk that your raw dough will form a crust as it proves. To avoid this, Andrew Whitley suggests placing it in a large clean plastic bag and inflating the bag so that it doesn't touch the dough. I usually cover the dough with a very large bowl, which acts like a cloche. The dough is ready when it gently resists being lightly pressed, but still springs back. It should feel fragile and alive. At which point, whisk it into the oven and feel deeply virtuous as your kitchen fills with the scent of freshly baked bread.

PIZZA DOUGH

Uncooked pizza dough freezes very well. This is a classic pizza dough, but you can blend different flours into the white flour, such as a quarter rye or wholemeal flour to add different flavours. See pages 149 and 239 for pizza and calzone recipes.

SERVES 4

225ml/8fl oz tepid water
2 teaspoons fast-action dried yeast

400g/14oz strong white flour
1 teaspoon salt

1 Place 3 tablespoons of tepid water in a small bowl. Sprinkle the yeast over the water and gently mix with your finger. Measure the flour into a large mixing bowl. Once the yeast has dissolved and looks frothy, mix thoroughly. Add 2 tablespoons of the measured flour and stir until it forms a smooth paste. Leave to rise for 30 minutes. It will fluff up and double in volume.

2 Mix the salt into the remaining flour. Pour in the yeast mixture. Add 225ml/8fl oz lukewarm water to the empty yeast bowl and then tip into the flour and yeast mixture. Using your hands, mix together until it forms a dough, then turn on to a clean surface.

3 Knead thoroughly for 10 minutes. Once the dough is silky smooth and elastic, divide into four equal balls. Place on a floured baking sheet. If possible, encase the baking sheet in an inflated clean plastic bag; otherwise, cover with a clean tea towel. Leave in a warm, draught-free place for 2 hours or until they've doubled in size.

4 Preheat your oven to its highest setting, which is usually around fan 230°C/gas 9. Taking one ball of dough at a time, knead for 2 minutes and then, using the palm of your hand, press out and flatten into a thin circle. You can use a small rolling pin to make it really thin, but press your knuckles just inside the edge to create a raised edge. If you're making a calzone, the edge should be slightly thicker.

5 Top the pizza or fill the calzone as suggested in your chosen recipe.

OLIVE OIL BREAD

This is a lovely, flat, Italian-style bread to bake on a summer's day. It tastes best eaten freshly baked, especially if served with a tomato salad.

MAKES A 450G/1LB LOAF

450g/1lb strong white flour
1 teaspoon fine sea salt
345ml/12fl oz tepid water
2 teaspoons fast-action dried yeast

5½ tablespoons extra virgin olive oil
55g/2oz pitted green olives, cut into chunks
1 teaspoon coarse sea salt

1 In a large bowl, mix together the flour and fine salt. Measure 200ml/7fl oz of the tepid water into a small bowl and sprinkle the yeast over the water. Leave for about 10 minutes or until it has dissolved and looks frothy, then stir and mix into the flour. Add the remaining water to the yeast bowl and tip into the flour. Mix until you have a soft dough, then turn on to a clean surface.

2 Knead the dough for about 10 minutes or until silky smooth. Flatten it out and indent with your fingers. Drizzle over 2 tablespoons of the olive oil. It will be very squelchy. Gently fold over the dough and knead to incorporate the oil. Repeat with another 2 tablespoons of oil. Add the olives and knead for 5 minutes or until the dough is smooth and supple.

3 Add 1 tablespoon of olive oil to a large bowl and add the dough, lightly coating it in the oil. Cover the bowl with clingfilm and leave in a warm, draught-free place for 2 hours or until the dough has doubled in size.

4 Turn out the dough and knead briefly. Shape into a large flattened circle about 2.5cm/1in thick and place on a heavy baking sheet. Cover with a large inverted bowl or place in an inflated plastic bag. Leave to rise for 1 hour or until soft and spongy.

5 Preheat the oven to fan 220°C/gas 8. Mix ½ tablespoon olive oil with ¼ teaspoon water. Make large indentations in the dough with your fingers, then brush with the oil and water. Sprinkle with the coarse sea salt, then bake for 12–15 minutes or until the bread is golden and sounds hollow when tapped on its bottom. Cool on a wire rack or take straight to the table.

MIXED GRAIN BREAD

This aromatic, crusty, mixed grain bread is really good with soup or cheese. Like all bread, it freezes well.

MAKES ONE FAMILY-SIZED LOAF

2 teaspoons fast-action dried yeast
300ml/10½ fl oz tepid water
500g/1lb 2oz stoneground malted blend flour

1½ teaspoons fine sea salt
15g/½ oz sunflower seeds
30g/1oz pumpkin seeds

1 Measure 100ml/3½ fl oz tepid water into a bowl. Sprinkle the yeast over the water, mix and leave for 10 minutes or until it has dissolved, smells of fresh yeast and looks frothy. In a large bowl mix together the flour, salt, sunflower seeds and 15g/½ oz of the pumpkin seeds. Add the frothy yeast, rinse the yeast bowl with 200ml/7fl oz tepid water and mix into the flour to form a supple dough. You may need to add more water, as different flours absorb different amounts of water.

2 Tip the dough on to a clean surface and knead for 10 minutes, until silky smooth and elastic. Place the dough in a mixing bowl. Cover with clingfilm and leave in a warm, draught-free place for 1 hour or until the dough has doubled in size.

3 Lightly dust a non-stick baking sheet with flour. Turn the dough on to a clean surface and knock back by briefly kneading, then shape into a torpedo. Scatter the remaining 15g/½ oz sunflower seeds on a large plate and firmly press the top of the dough on to the seeds, before squishing any remaining seeds into the bottom of the loaf. Place on the baking sheet and cover with a large inverted bowl or place in an inflated plastic bag. Leave to rise for 1 hour or until it has doubled in size.

4 Preheat the oven to fan 220°C/gas 8. When you are ready to bake, drop about 10 ice cubes into a wide ovenproof dish and place in the bottom of the preheated oven. At the same time, moisten the top of the loaf with water by running a wet hand along its crust. Bake for 20 minutes, then reduce the oven temperature to fan 200°C/gas 7. Bake for a further 20 minutes or until cooked. Check by tapping the bottom of the loaf: if it sounds hollow, it is cooked. Leave to cool on a wire rack.

COTEHELE MILL MASLIN BREAD

Maslin bread dates back to the Middle Ages and was the staple fare of servants and labourers. Millers and bakers across the land would mix their own blend of grains to make *masdeline* or *maslin* (from the Norman-French *miscelin*, meaning mixture). Typically, the mix would contain rye, barley and wheat flour. Only the very rich ate fine white wheat bread or *pandemain* (from *panis dominis*, 'lord's bread'). This recipe comes from the National Trust's Cotehele Mill in Cornwall, a Tudor watermill that still grinds local grain such as Maris Widgeon wheat. In Tudor times, barley would have been the principal grain for bread in Cornwall.

MAKES A 340G/12OZ LOAF

250ml/9fl oz tepid water
1 teaspoon fast-action dried yeast
1 teaspoon salt

100g/3½ oz rye flour
55g/2oz barley bread flour
170g/6oz stoneground wholemeal flour

1 Measure half the tepid water into a small bowl. Sprinkle the yeast over the water. Mix together the salt, rye, barley and stoneground flours in a large bowl. After about 10 minutes, once the yeast has dissolved and looks frothy, mix thoroughly and add to the flour. Rinse the yeast bowl with the remaining water and tip it into the flour. Using your hands, mix thoroughly until you have a soft dough.

2 Tip out on a clean surface and knead thoroughly for about 7 minutes. Place in a clean bowl and cover. Leave in a warm, draught-free place for 2–3 hours or until the dough has almost doubled in size.

3 Turn out and knock back by kneading for a few minutes. Shape into a round loaf and place on a non-stick baking sheet. Cut a cross in the top of the loaf and invert a large mixing bowl over it. It needs to have enough room to expand without touching the bowl. Alternatively, encase the baking sheet in an inflated plastic bag. Leave to rise for 1 hour or until it has doubled in size. Preheat the oven to fan 220°C/gas 8.

4 Bake for 20–25 minutes or until the loaf is golden brown and sounds hollow when tapped on its bottom. Leave to cool on a wire rack.

BUNS & ROLLS

There is something about buns that makes them irresistible to the English. In fact, they were so irresistible that we used to have bun houses dedicated to making sweet spicy fruit buns. Chelsea, Marylebone and Stepney in London became famous for their currant bun houses, although Jonathan Swift wasn't very impressed by the buns he bought from The Chelsea Bun Shop in 1711. They must have improved as both George II and George III became patrons, and later, Charles Dickens and Lewis Carroll mention the shop in their writings.

By the late eighteenth century, the leisured classes took to breakfasting on enriched spiced buns, washed down with the ultra-fashionable hot chocolate or coffee. Nor would anyone eschew a delicate white roll, a symbol of luxury.

Today, buns and rolls can be soft and savoury or sweet, fruited and sticky, it doesn't matter, so long as there are plenty of them. Luckily, they're very easy to make and freeze well. You can, of course, adapt any bread recipe to make rolls.

SOFT WHITE ROLLS

These gorgeous white rolls have a soft fluffy texture because they're made with milk. The better the quality of your plain white flour, the better the flavour of your rolls, so seek out local windmills and home-grown soft wheat such as Maris Widgeon. They're particularly good eaten warm with lots of butter.

MAKES 8 ROLLS

100ml/3½ fl oz tepid water
2 teaspoons fast-action dried yeast
500g/1lb 2oz organic plain white flour, plus extra
    for dusting

1½ teaspoons salt
170ml/6fl oz tepid full-fat milk, plus extra
    for glazing

1 Put the tepid water in a bowl, sprinkle the yeast over the water and mix thoroughly. Leave for 10 minutes or until it has dissolved, smells of fresh yeast and looks frothy. Mix the flour and salt in a large bowl. Add the frothy yeast, rinse the yeast bowl with the milk and mix into the flour. It should form a sticky dough, but if necessary add a little more tepid water as different flours will absorb different amounts of water.

2 Turn out on to a clean surface and knead for 10 minutes. Don't worry if it seems ridiculously sticky at first: it will become soft and silky as you knead it.

3 Place the dough in a clean bowl, cover with clingfilm and leave in a warm, draught-free place for 1 hour or until the dough has doubled in size. Knock back by briefly kneading, and leave to rest for 10 minutes.

4 Lightly dust two baking sheets with flour. Divide the dough into eight equal pieces. Roll each piece into a ball then gently shape each into a flat round about 1cm/½ in thick. Place on the baking sheets. Lightly brush each roll with milk and sift a little extra flour over each. Leave to rise, uncovered, for a further 30–45 minutes or until well risen and puffy. Preheat the oven to fan 200°C/gas 7.

5 Bake for 15 minutes or until well risen and lightly coloured. Tap the bottom of a roll: if it sounds hollow, it is cooked. Leave to cool on a wire rack. If you like your rolls really soft, cover with a tea towel while they cool. Be warned, these are very moreish.

WALNUT ROLLS

You can use any type of wholemeal flour here, from plain to a granary-style stoneground wholemeal flour that contains malted grain.

MAKES 8

300ml/10½ fl oz tepid water
2 teaspoons fast-action dried yeast
340g/12oz wholemeal flour (see above), plus
    extra for dusting

170g/6oz strong white flour
1 teaspoon fine sea salt
85g/3oz walnut halves, roughly chopped

1 Measure 100ml/3½ fl oz of the tepid water into a bowl, sprinkle the yeast over the water and leave for 10 minutes or until it has dissolved, smells of fresh yeast and looks frothy. Mix together the two flours and salt in a large bowl. Add the frothy yeast, rinse the yeast bowl with 200ml/7fl oz tepid water and mix into the flour to form a supple dough. Water quantities may vary as different flours absorb different amounts of water.

2 Turn out on to a clean surface and knead for 8 minutes, until the dough feels silky smooth and elastic.

3 Stretch out the dough and sprinkle on the walnuts. Press them into the dough, then roll up the dough and continue to knead, pushing any walnuts back into the dough as they pop out, until the nuts are evenly distributed throughout the dough. Place in a clean bowl, cover with clingfilm, and leave in a warm, draught-free place for about 2 hours or until the dough has doubled in size.

4 Lightly oil a baking sheet. Knock back the dough by briefly kneading, then divide into eight equal pieces. Shape each piece into a round or oblong roll. Lightly dust in flour and arrange on the baking sheet. Place the baking sheet in an inflated plastic bag. Leave to rise for a further 45 minutes or until well risen and puffy.

5 Preheat the oven to fan 200°C/gas 7. Bake for 15 minutes or until lightly coloured. Tap the bottom of a roll: if it sounds hollow, it is cooked. Leave to cool on a wire rack.

HOT CROSS BUNS

These buns can be frozen before or after baking. They're wonderful eaten warm or cold.

MAKES 6 BUNS

120ml/4fl oz full-fat milk
1 teaspoon fast-action dried yeast
250g/9oz strong white flour
½ teaspoon salt
1½ teaspoons mixed spice
½ teaspoon ground nutmeg
30g/1oz cold butter, diced
2 tablespoons caster sugar
30g/1oz currants
30g/1oz sultanas

30g/1oz chopped mixed peel
1 medium egg, beaten

PASTRY CROSS
30g/1oz plain flour, sifted
15g/½ oz butter, diced
1 teaspoon caster sugar

STICKY GLAZE
2 tablespoons full-fat milk
1½ tablespoons granulated sugar

1 Gently heat the milk until it is tepid. Pour half into a bowl and sprinkle with the yeast. Mix and leave for 10 minutes or until it has dissolved and looks frothy.

2 Sift the flour, salt and spices into a large bowl. Add the butter and, using your fingertips, rub it into the flour until it forms fine crumbs. Mix in the sugar, currants, sultanas and mixed peel. Make a well in the centre of the mixture and stir in the egg , yeasty milk and enough tepid milk to form a soft dough. It should not be too sticky – if it clings to your fingers, add a little more flour.

3 Turn the dough on to a clean surface. Knead thoroughly for 10 minutes. Place in a clean bowl. Cover with clingfilm. Leave to rise in a warm place for about 1½ hours, until the dough has risen by a third.

4 Lightly oil a baking sheet. Turn the dough out on to a clean surface and knead for a minute. Divide into six equal pieces. Shape each into a neat ball. Place on the baking sheet, flattening each ball slightly. Place in a plastic bag. Leave in a warm place for 45 minutes or until the buns look very puffy.

5 Preheat the oven to fan 200°C/gas 7. Once the buns are risen, make the pastry crosses. Sift the flour into a small bowl and, using your fingertips, rub in the butter until the mixture forms fine crumbs. Mix in the sugar, then stir in 1 tablespoon cold water to make a firm dough. Roll out on a floured work surface to about 3mm/⅛ in thick, then cut into strips that are 10cm/4in long and 5mm/¼ in wide. Brush the pastry strips with a little water and arrange, sticky-side down, in a cross on the top of each bun. Bake for 15 minutes, until golden brown.

6 Meanwhile, prepare the glaze by heating the milk and sugar in a small saucepan over a low heat for 5 minutes or until the sugar has dissolved. Then boil vigorously for 30 seconds and remove as soon as it looks syrupy. Once the buns are cooked, transfer to a wire rack and brush immediately with the hot glaze.

CHELSEA BUNS

Famed for their delicate flavour and lightness, Chelsea buns were reputedly first made at the Old Chelsea Bun House, not far from Ranelagh Gardens in London. The shop was still there when the Carlyles moved into their house in Cheyne Row in 1834. No doubt many of their literary visitors, such as Dickens, stopped off for the odd bun. This English classic is a favourite in many National Trust restaurants. In some matters, British taste never changes. If you don't have any honey, you can always use the milk-and-sugar glaze recipe for hot cross buns on page 123.

MAKES 9 BUNS

130ml/4½ fl oz full-fat milk
2 teaspoons fast-action dried yeast
225g/8oz plain flour
½ teaspoon salt
15g/½ oz cold butter, diced

FRUIT FILLING
85g/3oz mixed dried fruit

55g/2oz light muscovado sugar
1 teaspoon mixed spice
finely grated zest of 1 lemon
40g/1½ oz butter, melted and cooled

STICKY GLAZE
2 tablespoons honey

1 Gently heat the milk until it is tepid. Tip into a bowl and sprinkle the yeast over it. Leave for 10 minutes or until it has dissolved, smells of fresh yeast and looks frothy.

2 Sift the flour and salt into a large bowl. Add the butter and, using your fingertips, rub it into the flour until it forms fine crumbs. Mix in the yeasty milk. You should have a soft, but not wet, supple dough. If it is too stiff, add a little tepid water.

3 Turn out on to a clean surface and knead for 10 minutes until the dough feels silky smooth and elastic. Place in a clean large bowl and cover. Leave to rise for 1½ hours or until it has doubled in size.

4 Turn the dough out on to a clean surface. Lightly knead for a minute, then roll it into a 23 x 30cm/9 x 12in rectangle. In a bowl mix together the mixed dried fruit,

muscovado sugar, mixed spice and lemon zest. Brush the dough with the melted butter and spread the fruit mixture to within 2.5cm/1in of the longer edges. Roll up the dough from the long sides and press the join to seal.

5 Grease a 20cm/8in round cake tin. Cut the dough into nine slices and place them in the cake tin, cut side upwards (see photograph, page 119). Leave to rise in a large polythene bag in a warm place for about 30 minutes or until well risen and puffy. Preheat the oven to fan 200°C/gas 7.

6 Warm the honey over a low heat and pour over the puffy buns before placing them in the oven. Bake for about 25 minutes, until golden brown. Leave to cool on a wire rack.

THE KITCHEN GARDEN

THE KITCHEN GARDEN

Who can resist the romantic notion of stepping out on a dewy summer's morning to gather a basketful of peas or raspberries to inspire some delicate baked concoction?

In a world where the majority of the population now lives in cities, the idea of a rural idyll that supplies your every need is very powerful. The English kitchen garden has become an idealised symbol of self-sufficiency. The allotment garden is its twenty-first-century equivalent. But even the window sill of the tiniest urban flat can be used to grow pots of rosemary or lavender, ready to be snipped at a moment's notice for some fragrant bread or sugary shortbread.

Anyone who grows their own fruit and vegetables is instantly more in touch with the natural world. Every nuance in the weather and change in the surrounding biodiversity has an implication in the garden and consequently in the kitchen.

It may be impossible for many urban cooks to garden, but we can all remain linked to the seasons through our cooking. It can be a pleasure to search out British-grown produce in shops and farmers' markets, even though it sometimes takes time, energy and imagination. In April, for example, when there is little home-grown fruit on the market, you have to devise creative ways to use apples, pears, rhubarb, frozen berries and sweet root vegetables.

By entertaining such ideas, you will immediately become more in tune with the world around you. Allow yourself certain imports – after all, eighteenth-century aristocrats delighted in growing lemons, oranges and pineapples. Then start to develop your recipes to maximise your use of home-grown produce.

This leads you to look at baking from the perspective of ingredients. This chapter explores how to do that, by looking at the different sections of a traditional kitchen garden such as you might discover within the walls of Calke Abbey in Derbyshire, Chartwell in Kent or the seventeenth-century garden of Fenton House in London. Flowers and herbs, shoots, vegetables, soft fruit and roots – each have their role within a baking book. I've moved apricots, plums, greengages and cherries to the next chapter, although traditionally they were often trained along the warm brick wall of a kitchen garden.

Focusing your baking on home-grown produce, particularly for the non-gardener, is a challenge. In this chapter, I have suggested various ideas for you to pursue. By doing so, you will start to create the next phase of British cooking: a unique modern style that reflects its natural environment.

ABOVE LEFT Runner beans and peas in the walled kitchen garden at Arlington Court, Devon.

ABOVE RIGHT Pot marigolds amongst the vegetables in the kitchen garden at Chartwell, Kent.

FLOWERS & HERBS

English cooks have always used herbs and flowers to flavour their food. Over the centuries, they've candied, pickled, distilled, infused and baked everything from violets and clary sage flowers to marigolds and roses.

There are two main ways of flavouring baked dishes with herbs or flowers: first, by mixing them into a crust, topping, cake mixture or meringue; second, by infusing them in a liquid. The first exposes the herb or flower to a dry heat, the second to a wet heat.

Some herbs acquire an unpleasant 'dried' flavour when subjected to dry heat. Dry heat requires oil-rich herbs such as thyme, rosemary, marjoram and lavender. A teaspoon of finely chopped thyme mixed into a pastry dough, for example, adds a subtle herbal dimension to a savoury tart. A small amount of chopped rosemary or lavender folded into whisked egg whites creates a fragrant meringue.

A good way to flavour cakes with herbs is to finely blend the herb in a food processor with some caster sugar before beating with the butter. Its not worth making such sugars in advance as the flavour of the herb deteriorates. The one exception is lavender flower sugar. This is sold by some supermarkets and can be used when you have no lavender to hand.

Flowers tend to lose their natural oils very quickly when subjected to dry heat, so with one or two exceptions, namely lavender and pot marigolds, it is more effective to use other methods of imparting their flavour to 'dry heat' dishes. Traditionally, distilled rose or orange flower water was added to baked dishes. However, you can also add floral flavours to a dish after it has been cooked. An almond cake, for instance, can be drenched in homemade chamomile syrup, or a cream filling can be flavoured with crushed candied roses or

violets, such as in the chocolate violet éclairs on page 305.

Pot marigolds gained their name from the fact that they were added to stews and pottages (thick soups) in medieval times. They continued to be used as a flavouring and colouring by country cooks until the nineteenth century. Their petals have a saffron-like flavour, which works well in savoury baked dishes that contain butter, cream, eggs or cheese.

Infusing herbs and flowers in a warm liquid is an easy way to impart their aroma into creams, custards and fruit fillings that are then baked in a tart, pudding or gratin. For example, see rhubarb and elderflower charlotte on page 230 or tomato gratin on page 155. The warmth of the liquid helps to extract the plant oils, imbuing the dish with a lovely flavour. Take care to use both herbs and flowers in moderation. The art of cooking is to make the eater wonder at how such a delicious dish was created.

You should always wash herbs and flowers before use. It is safest only to use flowers from a known source to ensure that they haven't been sprayed with any pesticides. People don't expect you to go around eating their gorgeous damask roses, even though they are edible. The best way to wash flowers is to dip them into cool water, shake lightly and leave to dry on kitchen paper.

Syrups

Syrups are a wonderful way of imbuing baked dishes such as cakes and rum babas with a fresh flavour. Lemon verbena, chamomile, rosemary, sweet cicely, lemon thyme and scented geranium leaves (*Pelargonium*) all taste fabulous infused into a simple lemon and sugar syrup.

Flavoured syrups – to make a syrup for a 20cm/8in cake, place 30g/1oz granulated sugar in a non-corrosive saucepan with 100ml/3½ fl oz water and the finely pared zest of 1 lemon. Dissolve the sugar over a low heat and simmer the liquid for 10 minutes. Remove from the heat. Bruise the leaves of your chosen washed herb and stir into the piping-hot syrup. Leave until cold. If the flavour is too delicate, remove the herbs, reheat the liquid, add some fresh herbs and leave to cool. Add lemon juice to taste and strain.

Sugared flowers

Sugared flowers make a beautiful decoration for cakes and puddings. In springtime, use edible cultivated flowers such as primroses and sweet violets; in summer, think of roses or fragrant pinks (*Dianthus*).

The method is the same for any flower you choose to sugar, but I've included instructions for primroses and rose petals (below) as they are used for the lemon Victoria sandwich on page 33 and almond rose fairy cakes on page 137. You should always remove any green parts and the white heel of the petal – but as long as you don't eat those parts it doesn't

matter. If sugaring borage flowers, you should also remove the pistils and stamens for the best taste. I always use egg white to sugar my flowers, which means that the petals will only last a day or two.

Sugared primroses – gently dip your freshly picked primroses in a basin of cool water, then allow to dry on kitchen paper. When dry, brush the petals with beaten egg white then dust with caster sugar. Leave to dry on greaseproof paper.

Sugared rose petals – take a freshly picked, unsprayed rose. Ideally, it should be heavily scented, such as a damask rose or a *Rosa rugosa*. Separate the petals and snip off the white heel at the base of each petal. Beat a little egg white and, using a paint brush, delicately coat the first petal in egg white, before liberally dusting it with caster sugar. Lay out on some greaseproof paper to dry. Repeat with the remaining petals. The sugary coating needs to harden before use. This will take about 1 hour.

CHEESE AND MARIGOLD MUFFINS

These savoury muffins are best eaten on the day they're baked. The marigold petals are infused into the warm butter before baking. The orange and yellow petals will streak the muffins saffron yellow and add a slightly peppery note.

MAKES 10 MUFFINS

2 tablespoons pot marigold
   (*Calendula officinalis*) **petals**
115g/4oz butter
1 small onion, finely chopped
150ml/5fl oz cold full-fat milk

2 medium eggs, beaten
250g/9oz self-raising flour
½ teaspoon bicarbonate of soda
pinch of salt
30g/1oz Lancashire cheese, finely grated

1 Preheat the oven to fan 170°C/gas 4. Place 10 paper muffin cases in a muffin tray. Pull the petals off about 4 pot marigold heads and discard their centres; you need 2 tablespoons of petals.

2 Melt the butter in a small saucepan and gently fry the onion for 10 minutes or until soft and golden. Remove from the heat and mix in the marigold petals. Leave to cool slightly. Add the milk, followed by the eggs.

3 Sift the flour, bicarbonate of soda and salt into a large mixing bowl. Stir thoroughly, then mix in the grated cheese. Using a metal spoon, quickly fold in the warm milk and onion mixture, using as few strokes as possible. Do not over-mix.

4 Quickly spoon the mixture into the muffin cases and bake for 20–25 minutes, until golden and well risen. A skewer inserted into the centre should come out clean. Transfer to a wire rack and serve hot, warm or cold, with butter.

ALMOND ROSE FAIRY CAKES

In the eighteenth century, cooks regularly baked cakes flavoured with distilled rose or orange flower water. Today, it is important to buy a good-quality distilled rose water: the best are from the Middle East. These cakes keep well in an airtight container. You can buy crystallised rose petals if you can't find any unsprayed home-grown roses.

MAKES 12 FAIRY CAKES

ALMOND ROSE CAKES

115g/4oz butter, softened
115g/4oz caster sugar
1 tablespoon distilled rose water
1 teaspoon almond extract
2 medium eggs, lightly beaten
30g/1oz plain flour
115g/4oz ground almonds
1½ tablespoons full-fat milk

ROSE ICING

140g/5oz icing sugar
1 tablespoon distilled rose water
1 tablespoon lemon juice

DECORATION

sugared rose petals (see page 133)

1 Preheat the oven to fan 180°C/gas 5. Place 12 paper cupcake cases in a bun tray (see equipment notes, page 15). Don't use the larger paper muffin cases – they're too big.

2 To make the cakes, beat the butter and sugar together until pale and fluffy. Then gradually beat in the rose water and almond extract. Beat in about half the beaten eggs, then sift the flour over the mixture and beat in, followed by the remaining egg. Mix in the almonds, followed by the milk.

3 Spoon the mixture into the paper cases. Bake for 20 minutes or until the cakes are well risen and golden. Test by lightly pressing with your fingertip: the sponge will spring back if cooked. Transfer to a wire rack and leave until cold before icing.

4 While the cakes are cooking, make the sugared rose petals. They need to dry for about an hour.

5 To make the rose icing, sift the icing sugar into a bowl. Using a wooden spoon, stir in the rose water, followed by the lemon juice, until you have a thick, smooth icing. Drop a teaspoonful of icing on to the centre of the first cake and tilt the cake slightly so that the icing spreads out evenly over the surface of the cake. If it's very thick, spread with a wet knife. Repeat with the remaining cakes.

6 Once the icing begins to set, gently press a sugared rose petal or two onto each cake. Leave until the icing is firm.

ROSEMARY SHORTBREAD

The buttery nature of shortbread lends itself to being flavoured by herbs; instead of rosemary, try this with lavender or lemon thyme. Wash the herbs and dry thoroughly before use. I use a salad spinner before gently patting dry with kitchen paper. The orange zest brings out the spicy notes of rosemary, but you could also use lemon zest.

MAKES 12 BISCUITS

55g/2oz caster sugar, plus extra for dusting
1 teaspoon finely chopped rosemary leaves
115g/4oz butter, softened

finely grated zest of 1 orange
170g/6oz plain flour, sifted

1 Preheat the oven to fan 150°C/gas 2½. Lightly oil a baking sheet.

2 Put the sugar and rosemary in a food processor. Whiz until the rosemary is very finely chopped, then add the butter and orange zest and whiz until pale and creamy. Transfer to a large bowl. Beat in the flour until it forms a stiff dough.

3 Place the dough on a sheet of baking parchment and cover with another sheet. Gently press down with a rolling pin and roll out to 3–5mm/⅛–¼ in thick. Lift off the top sheet of paper and stamp out the biscuits with a 7cm/2¾ in diameter pastry cutter. Using a palette knife, lift them off the paper and carefully transfer to the baking sheet. Lightly squidge the remaining dough together and repeat the process.

4 Prick the biscuits with a fork and bake for 12 minutes or until tinged a very pale brown. Using a palette knife (they will still be soft), transfer to a wire rack and liberally dust with caster sugar. Serve once cool and crisp.

LAVENDER MERINGUES WITH PEACHES AND CREAM

Peaches were first grown in England in the thirteenth century. They were favoured by the nobility, despite the fact that the thirteenth-century chronicler Roger of Wendover suggested that King John died in 1216 from eating a surfeit of green peaches washed down by ale. By the eighteenth century, they were all the rage, which in turn led to commercial production in Sussex in the nineteenth century.

SERVES 8

LAVENDER MERINGUES
3 medium egg whites
170g/6oz caster sugar
½ tablespoon cornflour
1 tablespoon finely chopped lavender flowers
1 teaspoon white wine vinegar

PEACHES AND CREAM
285ml/10fl oz double cream
1 tablespoon icing sugar, or to taste
2 tablespoons lemon juice
6 ripe peaches

1 Preheat the oven to fan 140°C/gas 2. Line two baking sheets with baking parchment.

2 To make the lavender meringues, whisk the egg whites in a large, clean dry bowl until they form stiff peaks. Add a quarter of the caster sugar and whisk until the mixture is stiff and glossy, then gradually whisk in the remaining sugar until the mixture is very glossy. Finally, fold in the cornflour, lavender and vinegar.

3 Spoon 16 evenly spaced blobs of meringue on to the parchment-lined baking sheets. Bake for 15 minutes, then reduce the oven temperature to fan 130°C/gas 1 and cook for a further 30 minutes or until the meringues are crisp outside and gooey inside. Remove from the oven, peel off the baking paper and leave on a wire rack until cold.

4 For the peaches and cream, whip the cream until it forms soft peaks. Set aside. Put the icing sugar and lemon juice in a large bowl. Quarter the peaches and, if you wish, peel. Finely slice each quarter and mix into the sweetened lemon juice. Adjust the sweetness to taste.

5 Serve two meringues per person. Either fold the peaches into the whipped cream and spoon on to the meringues, or spoon the cream on to the meringues and top with the sugary peaches.

LEMON THYME DRIZZLE CAKE

This iced lemon cake is flecked green from the lemon thyme. You can adapt this recipe to rosemary, lavender or plain thyme in place of lemon thyme. Delicious on a summer's afternoon with a cup of tea.

SERVES 6

115g/4oz caster sugar
2 tablespoons finely chopped lemon thyme leaves
115g/4oz butter, softened
finely grated zest and juice of 1 lemon
2 large eggs, lightly beaten
170g/6oz self-raising flour, sifted
pinch of salt

LEMON THYME ICING
2 tablespoons finely chopped lemon thyme leaves
140g/5oz icing sugar, sifted
1 lemon

DECORATION
sprigs of lemon thyme, with flowers if available

1 Preheat the oven to fan 170°C/gas 4. Grease a 450g/1lb loaf tin, line the base and ends with a strip of baking parchment and lightly grease the parchment.

2 Make sure the lemon thyme leaves are dry before you chop them. Then put in a food processor with the caster sugar and whiz until the sugar turns green and the leaves are finely chopped. Add the butter and lemon zest and whiz until fluffy, then gradually add the eggs. Mix in 1 tablespoon lemon juice, then scrape into a bowl and fold in the flour and salt.

3 Spoon into the prepared loaf tin. Bake in the oven for 20 minutes, then loosely cover the top with foil if it is browning too quickly and bake for a further 20–25 minutes or until well risen and golden. Test by inserting a skewer into the cake: if it comes out clean, the cake is cooked.

4 To make the icing, stir the finely chopped lemon thyme into the icing sugar and add enough lemon juice to form a thick icing.

5 Transfer the cake in its tin to a wire rack. Leave for 5 minutes, then remove from the tin and spoon the icing over the top of the warm cake. It will drizzle down the sides of the cake. Leave to cool. Shortly before serving, decorate with a few sprigs of lemon thyme.

SHOOTS

From the first frilly shoots of rhubarb in the spring until the first hard frost of winter, every kitchen garden and farmers' market is filled with an array of tempting shoots and leaves. Succulent asparagus, salad leaves, spring onions, leeks and chicory (Belgian endive) – the list is endless. Early in the season, such foods are easy to prepare. Who doesn't want to eat the first rhubarb fool or watercress soup of the year? But as each season stretches on, the skill of the cook is tested. How to ensure that rhubarb remains tempting week after week, and that leeks are as alluring in March as they were at the start of their season in September?

Happily, baking allows cooks to think laterally. Take asparagus as an example. It tastes good baked in a custard tart, so it might also be good puréed in a custard and baked in a similar way to the baked pea custards on page 157. Since asparagus is delicious when cooked in buttery pastry, it will also work well in a simple adaptation of the easy leek tart on page 144. This approach can be applied to any ingredient.

It is also helpful to analyse the texture and taste of your chosen food. With tender leaves such as spinach or watercress, you might like to highlight their raw texture by serving them uncooked with a baked item, such as the rocket-topped onion olive pizza on page 149, or you can transform their texture by cooking. Blanched spinach, for example, can be used as a tart filling or gratin, or puréed for a baked custard or soufflé (see page 156).

The sour taste of cooked rhubarb perfectly counterbalances rich sweet foods, so it will always taste good with ultra-sweet dishes such as the soft meringue roulade on page 151. Similarly, the bitter taste of chopped fresh watercress brings out the savoury sweetness of a cheese roulade when used in its cream cheese filling.

EASY LEEK TART

This style of tart works well with other vegetables such as blanched asparagus, sautéed onions, or blanched, quartered and lightly griddled chicory (Belgian endive). If you buy ready-made pastry, choose a butter puff pastry; you will need to buy a packet weighing about 370g/13oz. Interestingly, some artisan cheese-makers are now trying to create a British taleggio-style cheese.

SERVES 6

225g/8oz puff pastry (see page 84)
680g/1½ lb untrimmed leeks
½ tablespoon chopped fresh tarragon

salt and freshly ground black pepper
225g/8oz taleggio cheese

1 On a lightly floured surface, roll out the pastry into a large rectangle about 3mm/⅛ in thick. Using a 20 x 30cm/8 x 12in Swiss roll tin as a giant pastry cutter, cut out a rectangle of that size. If you are using homemade puff pastry there will be quite a lot of leftover pastry, so carefully fold up the trimmings and freeze. Take a sharp knife and lightly run it about 1cm/½ in inside the pastry edge, so that you score a line to create a rim for the tart. Prick the internal rectangle with a fork. Place on a non-stick baking sheet and chill for 30 minutes. Preheat the oven to fan 200°C/gas 7.

2 Trim the leeks of their roots and darker green leaves. Remove the tough outer leaves then slice lengthways through the green-coloured section of leaves. Wash thoroughly in a sink of cold water. Bring a pan of water to the boil. Add the leeks, return to the boil and cook briskly for 5 minutes or until just tender. Drain and cool under the cold tap. Squeeze out the excess water and pat dry on kitchen paper.

3 Slice the leeks and spread them over the pastry, taking care not to cover the rim. Scatter with the chopped tarragon and lightly season. Remove the rind from the cheese and slice or break into pieces. Dot over the filling.

4 Bake for 20 minutes or until the pastry is crisp and the cheese is bubbling and flecked gold.

ASPARAGUS TART

Traditionally, the British asparagus season runs from the end of April to the end of May. However, English farmers are developing new techniques, and it is not uncommon to find English asparagus in early April or late June.

SERVES 6

225g/8oz shortcrust pastry (see page 80)
2 tablespoons cold-pressed rapeseed oil
1 medium onion, finely chopped
250g/9oz asparagus
salt and freshly ground black pepper

1 medium egg
1 medium egg yolk
200ml/7fl oz double cream
30g/1oz Cheshire cheese, finely grated

1 Roll out the pastry on a lightly floured surface and line a 20cm/8in quiche dish. Prick the base of the pastry, line with greaseproof paper or foil and fill with baking beans. Chill for 30 minutes. Preheat the oven to fan 180°C/gas 5.

2 Bake the pastry case for 15 minutes, then remove the paper or foil and beans and return to the oven for a further 5 minutes.

3 While the pastry is cooking, place a non-stick frying pan over a medium heat. Add the oil and once hot, gently fry the onion for 10 minutes or until soft and golden.

4 Trim the stalks of the asparagus and wash thoroughly in a sinkful of cold water. Then drop them into a pan of unsalted boiling water. Cook for 3–4 minutes or until tender. Drain and cool under the cold tap. Pat dry on kitchen paper. Cut off the tips. Finely slice the stems and add to the softened onions, along with the tips. Season to taste. Spoon into the pastry case.

5 Beat together the egg, egg yolk and cream. Season to taste and pour into the pastry case. Sprinkle with the cheese and bake for 30 minutes or until golden and set. Serve warm or cold.

LEEK AND BACON FROISE

Froise, sometimes spelt fraise, dates back to the fifteenth century. Food was coated in a batter and cooked in the hot fat and juices that collected beneath a spit-roasted joint. These are lovely eaten for lunch or supper, followed by a salad, but are also good eaten as an accompaniment to roast chicken. They're quite filling, so if serving with roast chicken, you'll only need one per person. You can, of course, use other ingredients to flavour them, such as sautéed onions with blanched asparagus or peas.

MAKES 12

170g/6oz plain flour
pinch of salt
3 medium eggs, lightly beaten
200ml/7fl oz semi-skimmed milk
3 tablespoons cold-pressed rapeseed oil

225g/8oz smoked back bacon, trimmed of fat and
    finely diced
3 fat leeks
freshly ground black pepper

1 Sift the flour and salt into a bowl. Make a well in the centre and, using a wooden spoon, slowly beat in the eggs, followed by the milk, until you have a smooth batter. Give it a through beating, then leave to rest for 1 hour.

2 Preheat the oven to fan 200°C/gas 7. Place a non-stick 12-hole muffin tray in the oven.

3 Trim the leeks of their roots and dark leaves. Slice in half lengthways and remove any tough outer leaves. Wash thoroughly in cold water. Allow to drain, then finely slice.

4 Set a non-stick frying pan over a medium-high heat. Add the oil and once hot, add the bacon. Stir-fry briskly for 2 minutes or until lightly coloured, then reduce the heat slightly and mix in the leeks. Fry briskly for about 8 minutes or until they collapse, soften and release any excess liquid. Season to taste.

5 Quickly divide the leek mixture between the 12 preheated muffin moulds, then divide the batter between the 12 moulds. Immediately return to the oven and cook for 20–25 minutes or until the froise is well risen and golden. Serve hot or warm.

ROCKET-TOPPED ONION OLIVE PIZZA

Traditionally, pizza is cooked in a wood oven, so you need to heat your domestic oven to its maximum temperature. I put the pizza on a preheated heavy baking sheet, but you could use a pizza stone. You can prepare all the ingredients in advance.

SERVES 2

½ quantity pizza dough (see page 112)
125g/4½ oz buffalo mozzarella
2 tablespoons extra virgin olive oil, plus extra
    for sprinkling
2 medium onions, finely sliced
salt and freshly ground black pepper

2 tablespoons capers
10 large green or black olives, stoned and sliced
2 handfuls flat-leafed parsley leaves, roughly
    chopped
4 tablespoons finely grated Parmesan
2 large handfuls (40g/1½ oz) wild rocket, washed

1 Place a heavy baking sheet or pizza stone in the centre of your cold oven. Preheat the oven to fan 230°C/gas 9.

2 Drain the mozzarella and pat dry. Slice and place in a sieve over a bowl to release some of the excess moisture. This stops the pizza from becoming soggy. Lightly cover with clingfilm and chill.

3 Set a non-stick frying pan over a medium heat. Add the olive oil and once hot, fry the sliced onions gently for 10 minutes or until soft but not coloured. Season to taste and set aside, covered.

4 Rinse the capers, pat dry and place in a bowl with the olives. Mix in the parsley. Cover and chill.

5 When you're ready to cook, roll out your pizza dough as described on page 112. (Remember you are making two pizzas rather than four.) Slip the first one on to an oiled non-stick 20cm/8in cake tin base. Scatter half the onions over the pizza, keeping the rim free. Top with half the capers, olives and parsley leaves. Drizzle over a little more olive oil. Arrange half the slices of mozzarella over the pizza, scatter with half the Parmesan and then, using the cake base as pizza shovel, transfer to the hot baking sheet in the oven, leaving space for the second pizza. Working quickly, re-oil the cake base and repeat the process to make a second pizza.

6 Bake both for 12 minutes or until the dough is crisp and the mozzarella melted and flecked gold-brown. Remove and top with the wild rocket. Serve immediately.

RHUBARB TARTLETS

In the nineteenth century, rhubarb and gooseberry tarts were the cupcakes of their day. Choose slender stems of rhubarb for these pretty tarts. The recipe makes excess syrup, but you can keep it in a clean, sealed container in the fridge or freezer. Use it for mixed berry fruit salad or other rhubarb dishes. You can make gooseberry tarts in the same way.

SERVES 8

butter for greasing
225g/8oz shortcrust pastry (see page 80)
200ml/7fl oz water

200g/7oz granulated sugar
450g/1lb trimmed rhubarb, washed and cut into
    2.5cm/1in lengths

1 Butter eight 9cm/3½ in tartlet tins. On a lightly floured surface, roll out the pastry thinly and line the tart tins. Prick the bottoms with a fork, line with greaseproof paper or foil and fill with baking beans. Chill for 30 minutes. Preheat the oven to fan 180°C/gas 5.

2 Bake the tartlets for 15 minutes, or until the pastry begins to colour. Remove the foil and return to the oven to dry out for a further 5 minutes.

3 Meanwhile, put the water and sugar in a wide non-corrosive saucepan and set over a high heat until the sugar has dissolved. Place a single layer of rhubarb in the syrup and simmer gently for 4–5 minutes or until

it begins to soften, but still retains its shape. Carefully remove from the syrup with a slotted spoon and spread in a single layer on a large plate. Repeat with the remaining rhubarb. Once you've cooked all the rhubarb, vigorously boil the poaching syrup until it is very thick and syrupy. Do not let it caramelise.

4 Arrange the rhubarb in the pastry cases and spoon over some of the thickened syrup. Return to the oven and bake for a further 8–10 minutes, until it is lightly coloured. Serve warm or at room temperature, with thick double cream.

RASPBERRY RHUBARB ROULADE ^{GF}

This soft meringue roulade is for the sweet-toothed and is a good way to use up excess egg whites. You can halve the quantities and use a 20 x 30cm/ 8 x 12in Swiss roll tin if you only want to serve 4.

SERVES 8

RHUBARB CREAM
200g/7oz trimmed rhubarb, cut into chunks
40g/1½ oz granulated sugar
170ml/6fl oz double cream
400g/14oz raspberries

MERINGUE ROULADE
8 medium egg whites
340g/12oz caster sugar
2 teaspoons white wine vinegar
2 teaspoons cornflour
icing sugar for dusting

1 To make the rhubarb cream filling, place the rhubarb in a non-corrosive pan with 2 tablespoons water and the sugar. Cover and set over a low heat. Once the sugar has dissolved, stir thoroughly and simmer gently for about 10 minutes or until the rhubarb is meltingly soft. Remove from the heat, purée and leave until cold.

2 In a large bowl, whisk the double cream until it forms soft peaks. Fold in the rhubarb purée and chill, covered, until needed.

3 Preheat the oven to fan 140°C/gas 2. Cut a piece of 27 x 38cm/11 x 15in baking parchment slightly larger than a shallow baking tin. Lightly oil the tin, fold each edge of the baking parchment so that it forms a 2.5cm/1in rim. Snip each corner so that it stands up above the tin. Press the paper into the tin, secure with paper clips and lightly but meticulously brush with oil.

4 To make the meringue roulade, whisk the egg whites until they form stiff peaks, then gradually beat in the caster sugar until the mixture is thick and glossy. Using a metal spoon, fold in the vinegar and cornflour. Spread the mixture smoothly and evenly in the prepared tin, making sure there are no hidden air pockets by giving the tin a couple of sharp taps. Bake for 12–15 minutes, until soft and marshmallow-like.

5 Leave to rest in the tin for 5 minutes. Liberally dust a large sheet of baking parchment with sifted icing sugar. Lightly peel away the baking paper from the sides of the roulade and gently tip onto the icing-sugared parchment. Peel away the baking paper and leave to cool for 10 minutes.

6 Spread the chilled rhubarb cream over the meringue. Cover with the raspberries, gently pressing them into the cream. Using the parchment, tightly roll up the longer side of the meringue. Slip on to a baking sheet and chill for 3 hours.

7 Unwrap the roulade, trim the ends and slice to serve.

VEGETABLES

For centuries country cooks would inspect their garden or consult with the gardener before deciding what to make that week. Just as today, there were periods when the household was faced by a glut of produce. The array of vegetables may have changed over the years, but the question remains the same: how to ensure that nothing is wasted.

Baking is often neglected as a way of preparing vegetables, yet it lends itself to a wide range of delicious vegetable-based dishes. It is best to start with you chosen vegetable and then consider which method would enhance it. As a rough guide, vegetable-baking methods can be divided as follows: roasts, gratins, pies, pizzas and pastries, tarts, batters, custards and soufflés.

Roasted vegetables, such as red onions, garlic, tomatoes and butternut squash, have become very popular cooked with olive oil and herbs (see also Roots on page 170). Baked stuffed vegetables are a variation of roasted vegetables and include stuffed peppers, courgettes, marrow and squash. Stuffings range from sautéed vegetables and breadcrumbs to savoury rice and spiced mincemeat.

Many vegetables taste gorgeous in cheesy gratins, even blanched green cabbages, when mixed with sautéed onions, bacon and cannellini beans. At their simplest, you can blanch your chosen vegetable and top with some grated or sliced cheese.

Equally irresistible is the contrast between soft luscious vegetables and crisp pastry or pizza dough, especially when presented in the form of little filo parcels or savoury turnovers.

Throughout the pages of this book you will find examples for tarts, batters, custards and soufflés that you can adapt to your needs, including a sweet cinnamon pumpkin pie on page 53 and leek and bacon froise on page 147.

TOMATO GRATIN

As late summer comes around, many gardener cooks are inundated with tomatoes. You can use this recipe for other types of tomatoes and different herbs, such as tarragon or thyme. By simmering the cream, you stop it splitting when it mixes with the acidic tomato juice as it bakes. Try serving with grilled white fish or chicken, and crusty bread.

SERVES 4

butter for greasing
285ml/10fl oz double cream
2 sprigs basil

salt and freshly ground black pepper
3 beef tomatoes
2 tablespoons finely grated Cheddar

1 Preheat the oven to fan 200°C/gas 7. Lightly butter a shallow gratin dish.

2 Put the cream and basil in a small saucepan and simmer gently until the cream has thickened and reduced by half, then strain into a jug and season to taste.

3 Neatly cut out the tough white core beneath the stem of each tomato and cut a small cross on the bottom. Place in a bowl, cover with boiling water for a few seconds, then quickly cool and peel. Slice into 1cm/½ in thick rounds.

4 Layer the tomatoes in the buttered dish. Lightly season each layer Pour over the reduced cream, sprinkle with cheese, and bake for 20 minutes or until bubbling hot and speckled golden. Serve warm.

SPINACH SOUFFLÉ

Soufflés are surprisingly easy to make. For an even rise and a stable soufflé, you need to gently and carefully fold the whisked egg whites into a relatively thick, tepid sauce.

If you're using large leafy spinach, as opposed to the tender leaves you find in supermarkets, you'll need to remove the tough rib by folding the leaf vertically so that the stem runs down one side and pulling the stem away, so that you're left with two pieces of leaf without any stem attached.

SERVES 4 AS A STARTER OR 2 AS A MAIN COURSE

35g/1¼ oz butter, plus extra for greasing
1½ tablespoons freshly grated Parmesan
300ml/10½ fl oz full-fat milk
1 bay leaf
35g/1¼ oz plain flour
400g/14oz fresh spinach, washed

5 medium egg yolks
55g/2oz strong Cheddar, finely grated
pinch of cayenne pepper
freshly grated nutmeg
salt and freshly ground black pepper
6 medium egg whites

1 Remove the top rack from the oven. Preheat the oven to fan 180°C/gas 5. Butter a 1.5 litre/2½ pint soufflé dish, then dust with the Parmesan cheese.

2 Put the milk and bay leaf in a small pan and scald by bringing to just below boiling point, then remove from the heat. Melt 35g/1¼ oz butter in a pan over a low heat. Using a wooden spoon, stir in the flour and cook for 1 minute. Slowly add the hot milk, stirring all the time to make a smooth sauce. Simmer gently, stirring occasionally, for 5 minutes. Remove from the heat and set aside for 10 minutes. Remove the bay leaf. The sauce should be relatively thick, but should drop from a spoon without any effort on your part.

3 Drop the spinach into a pan of unsalted boiling water. As soon as it has wilted – a few seconds – drain into a colander and cool under cold running water. Drain and squeeze dry. Measure out 225g/8oz cooked spinach and finely chop.

4 Mix the chopped spinach into the white sauce, followed by the egg yolks, grated cheese, cayenne pepper and nutmeg to taste. Season liberally and leave to cool slightly.

5 Once the sauce is tepid, put the egg whites in a large clean dry bowl and whisk until they form soft peaks. Using a metal spoon, fold a large dollop of whisked white into the cheese sauce to loosen it. Gently fold in the remaining egg whites.

6 Immediately tip into the prepared soufflé dish and level the top with a spoon. Place in the centre of the oven and bake for 25 minutes. If you like a wobbly soufflé, test at this stage by inserting a thin skewer. The soufflé should have a slightly soft centre and will leave a little of its sauce on the skewer. If you prefer a firmer soufflé, cook for 5–10 more minutes. Serve immediately.

BAKED PEA CUSTARDS

When bags of fresh peas are for sale in July, most town dwellers find them irresistible. If you can restrain yourself from eating the raw peas, they make a lovely savoury custard. Try serving these for lunch with crusty bread and a pretty leaf salad.

SERVES 6

500g/1lb 2oz fresh (shelled) or frozen peas
4 tablespoons finely grated Cheshire cheese
250ml/9fl oz double cream

5 medium eggs
salt and freshly ground black pepper

1 Preheat the oven to fan 180°C/gas 5. Lightly oil six 150ml/5fl oz ramekin dishes and place on some kitchen paper in a deep roasting pan.

2 Drop the peas into a pan of unsalted boiling water, return to the boil, cover and reduce to a simmer. Cook for 7 minutes or until meltingly tender, then drain and tip into a food processor. Add the cheese and process until smooth. Add the cream and eggs, and process until they're thoroughly mixed into the purée. Season to taste.

3 Divide the mixture evenly between the ramekins. Pour enough boiling water into the roasting pan to come halfway up the sides of the dishes and cover the roasting pan with foil. Bake for 30 minutes or until just set. Serve warm.

BROAD BEAN, FETA AND SAGE CROSTINI

Serve these as a nibble with drinks. They really taste of summer and are an excellent way of using up slightly tough broad beans and slightly stale bread. You can make both the crostini and the topping in advance.

MAKES ABOUT 20 CROSTINI

½ sourdough baguette
1 fat clove garlic, cut in half
1–2 tablespoons extra virgin olive oil

BROAD BEAN TOPPING
200g/7oz shelled broad beans
1 small clove garlic, finely chopped

2 teaspoons finely shredded sage leaves
4 tablespoons extra virgin olive oil
85g/3oz barrel-cured feta cheese, crumbled
1–2 tablespoons lemon juice
salt and freshly ground black pepper

1 Preheat the oven to fan 180°C/gas 5. Cut the bread into about twenty 1cm/½ in thick slices. Rub with the cut clove of garlic and drizzle with olive oil. Place on a baking sheet and bake for 10 minutes or until crisp and golden. Cool on a wire rack. Once cold, store the crostini in an airtight tin if not using within a few hours.

2 To make the topping, drop the broad beans into a pan of boiling water. Return to the boil, cover and simmer for 2–3 minutes or until tender, then drain and cool under cold running water. Pop each bean out of its pale green skin to reveal the bright green inner kernel.

3 If you have a pestle and mortar, gently crush the broad bean kernels, in batches, aiming for a crumbly, rough texture rather than a smooth paste. Transfer to a mixing bowl. Put the garlic, sage and 1 tablespoon of olive oil in the mortar. Gently crush and mix into the broad beans. Mix in the crumbled feta cheese. Add lemon juice to taste, along with the remaining olive oil. Season to taste. If not serving immediately, cover and chill.

4 If you don't have a pestle and mortar, roughly crush the beans with a potato masher, and crush the garlic and sage with the back of a spoon.

5 Shortly before you're ready to serve, bring the broad bean mixture up to room temperature and spoon on to your crostini.

SOFT FRUIT

In the sixteenth century, doctors believed that eating raw fruit caused nasty fevers. Nevertheless, many still indulged, as Andrew Boorde records in 1542: 'Raw creame eaten with strawberries or hurtes [whortleberries] is a rurall mans banquet.' He warns, however, 'I have known such banquets hath put men in jeopardy of their lives.' As a result, soft fruit such as strawberries, raspberries, gooseberries and currants were often cooked and served in pottages, pies or tarts. This tradition continued until quite recently.

Cooking soft fruit intensifies its sweet-sour flavour. This can be used to enhance sweet, rich baked dishes such as blackcurrant meringue pie (see page 49) or elderflower and gooseberry curd cake (see page 44). In the eighteenth century, cooks would often enrich a fruit pie by pouring in a caudle (custard) of boiled cream mixed with egg yolks through a funnel into the pie, shortly before the end of baking. This thickened the intense-tasting raspberry, gooseberry or currant juice under the crust.

Today, raw berries are very fashionable served in tarts, roulades, pavlovas and cream cakes. Delicious as they all are, and you will find plenty of such recipes scattered through the pages of this book, if you are keen to cook British-grown food throughout the year, it is worth developing cooked berry dishes. All you need to do is ensure that you freeze fresh raspberries, gooseberries, black and red currants when they're in season. This is especially important for town dwellers as, sadly, supermarkets don't see fit to sell frozen gooseberries or blackcurrants, despite the fact that they freeze well. They can be added frozen to dishes such as the raspberry Bakewell cake on page 163 or the gooseberry cream pie on page 167. If you want to freeze strawberries, they'll need to be either puréed or partially cooked with another fruit such as apples, as they don't freeze well raw when whole.

STRAWBERRY LAVENDER EVE'S PUDDING

Traditionally, Eve's pudding is made by baking a layer of chopped apples covered with a sponge mixture – which could be flavoured with lemon and vanilla. Over the years, I've experimented by combining all manner of fruit under the sponge topping. Many summer berries, such as strawberries, raspberries or blueberries, taste delicious, expecially when combined with apple, although you could try rhubarb instead. Such mixtures are wonderful flavoured with lavender or rosemary. This pudding can be served hot, warm or at room temperature.

SERVES 6

3 Bramley apples
115g/4oz granulated sugar
450g/1lb strawberries
1 tablespoon chopped lavender flowers,
    plus 3 sprigs

115g/4oz caster sugar, plus extra for sprinkling
115g/4oz butter, softened
2 medium eggs, beaten
115g/4oz self-raising flour, sifted

1 Preheat the oven to fan 180°C/gas 5. Peel, core and roughly chop the apples. Mix with the granulated sugar in a large bowl. Wash, hull and halve the strawberries. Mix into the apples and tip into a deep 1.8kg/4lb pie dish. Tuck 3 lavender sprigs into the fruit.

2 Place the lavender flowers in a food processor with the caster sugar. Whiz until the lavender is finely chopped. Don't worry if it looks a bit mauve! Add the butter and process until fluffy. Transfer to a bowl and beat in the eggs, a little at a time, adding a spoonful of flour if the mixture begins to separate. Finally, fold in the flour. Spoon the mixture in blobs over the fruit.

3 Immediately place in the centre of the oven. Bake for 50 minutes or until golden and risen; the sponge should spring back if lightly pressed. Serve with lots of cream.

RASPBERRY BAKEWELL CAKE

The National Trust usually make this lovely gooey pudding with ground almonds, but it is also delicious made with ground hazelnuts, as here. It's a great way of using up over-ripe or frozen raspberries. If using ground almonds, just add all the ingredients at the same time to the food processor and scatter with 2 tablespoons of flaked almonds.

SERVES 8

140g/5oz blanched hazelnuts
140g/5oz self-raising flour
140g/5oz butter, softened
140g/5oz unrefined caster sugar
2 medium eggs

½ teaspoon vanilla extract
250g/9oz raspberries
2 tablespoons finely sliced blanched hazelnuts
1 tablespoon icing sugar

1 Preheat the oven to fan 170°C/gas 4. Lightly oil a 20cm/8in spring-form cake tin. Line the base with baking parchment and lightly oil.

2 Put the hazelnuts in the food processor with the flour and whiz until the nuts are finely ground (the same consistency as shop-bought ground almonds). Add the butter, caster sugar, eggs and vanilla and process until well mixed.

3 Spread half the mixture into the cake tin and smooth the top. Scatter the raspberries over the surface. Dollop the remaining cake mixture over the raspberries and roughly spread – use your fingers if necessary. Scatter the surface with sliced blanched hazelnuts and bake for 35–40 minutes or until golden.

4 Leave to cool in the tin on a wire rack. Once cool, remove from the tin and sift a dusting of icing sugar over the cake.

RASPBERRY ALMOND TART

This is in the modern style, with fresh berries on top of a frangipane mixture.

SERVES 6

225g/8oz rich shortcrust pastry (see page 82)

FRANGIPANE FILLING
100g/3½ oz butter, softened
100g/3½ oz caster sugar
few drops of almond extract

2 medium eggs, beaten
100g/3½ oz ground almonds

RASPBERRY TOPPING
340g/12oz raspberries
½ tablespoon icing sugar, sifted

1 Preheat the oven to fan 180°C/gas 5. Roll out the pastry and line a 20cm/8in tart tin with a removable base. Prick the pastry with a fork, line with greaseproof paper or foil and fill with baking beans. Chill for 30 minutes.

2 Bake the pastry case for 15 minutes. Remove the paper and beans, and bake for a further 5 minutes. Remove from the oven and reduce the oven temperature to fan 170°C/gas 4. Leave to cool slightly.

3 To make the frangipane filling, beat together the butter, sugar and almond extract until pale and fluffy, then gradually beat in the eggs. Finally, mix in the almonds. Spoon into the cool pastry case and bake for 15–20 minutes or until the almond filling is golden and slightly risen. Don't overcook or the filling will be too dry.

4 Remove to a wire rack. Once cool enough to handle comfortably, remove from tin. Leave until cold.

5 Cover the almond filling with a tightly packed, single layer of raspberries, all sitting pointed side up. Dust with icing sugar before serving.

GOOSEBERRY CREAM PIE

In the eighteenth century, fruit pies were often enriched with a caudle, a warm mixture of cream and eggs that was poured into the pie crust. This is a simpler variation. If you happen to have elderflowers available, infuse them in the cream as it simmers or tuck them in with the gooseberries. In either case, take care to fish out the elderflower stems when serving. You can use frozen gooseberries.

SERVES 4

285ml/10fl oz double cream
150g/5½ oz granulated sugar, plus 1 tablespoon
    for sprinkling

500g/1lb 2oz gooseberries, topped and tailed
225g/8oz puff or rough puff pastry (see page 83–84)
1 small egg white, beaten

1 Pour the cream into a heavy-bottomed saucepan and simmer gently until it has thickened and reduced by almost half. This prevents it from splitting later. Stir in the sugar and leave to cool slightly.

2 Once the cream is tepid, stir in the gooseberries and, if necessary, adjust the sweetness to taste.

3 Roll out the pastry on a lightly floured surface. Using the top of the pie dish as a template cut out the pastry lid, making it 1cm/½ in larger to allow for the pie funnel. Now roll out the trimmings and cut a 1cm/½ in ribbon. Press firmly on to the rim of your pie dish. Brush this with egg white.

4 Spoon the creamy gooseberries into the pie dish and slip in a pie funnel. Loosely roll the pastry lid around the rolling pin, lift over the pie dish and unroll. Using a fork, press firmly around the rim so that the pastry lid is 'glued' to the rim. If necessary, cut off the excess pastry, using a sharp knife.

5 Prick the lid in three places with a small sharp knife and brush with egg white. You can roll out the trimmings to decorate the pie. Brush the pastry decoration with egg white and liberally sprinkle with granulated sugar. It can be chilled at this stage.

6 Preheat the oven to fan 180°C/gas 5. Bake the pie for 35 minutes or until the pastry is crisp and golden. Serve hot, warm or cold.

SUMMER BERRY CREAM PUFFS

These make a wonderful summer pudding, but are also popular at teatime. You can vary the fruit filling according to what you have to hand.

MAKES 24 PUFFS

choux pastry (see page 85)

SUMMER BERRY FILLING
115g/4oz red currants
300g/10½ oz raspberries
285ml/10fl oz double cream

2 tablespoons Grand Marnier
2–3 tablespoons icing sugar, or to taste

CARAMEL
115g/4oz granulated sugar
4 tablespoons water

1 To make the choux puffs, follow the recipe on page 85, but cook for 25 minutes or until golden and crisp. Then continue as instructed for cream puffs in the choux pastry recipe.

2 Once the puffs are cold, prepare the filling. Wash the currants, gently pat dry on kitchen paper, and strip from their stems. Place in a bowl with the raspberries.

3 Put the cream, Grand Marnier and icing sugar in a large bowl. Whisk until the cream forms soft peaks, then fold in the fruit.

4 Cut a slit into the side of each choux puff and, using a teaspoon, spoon the cream mixture into the puffs. Return them to the cooling rack and place a sheet of greaseproof paper underneath to catch the caramel drips.

5 To make the caramel, put the sugar and water in a small heavy-bottomed saucepan over a low heat until the sugar has dissolved. Then increase the heat and boil rapidly – without stirring – until it turns a beautiful golden caramel. It will continue to darken after it's off the heat, so take it off shortly before you think it's the right colour. Using a teaspoon, gently drizzle the hot caramel over the top of the puffs, taking care not to pour it over the cream, as this will melt with the heat. Leave the caramel to cool and harden for about 30 minutes, then serve.

ROOTS

In recent years, it's become very fashionable to bake cakes with root vegetables, in particular, carrots and beetroot. The latter is usually combined with chocolate. This is nothing new: root vegetables have come in and out of fashion since late Tudor times. At that time, cooks could choose from all manner of interesting roots, including carrots, beetroot, turnips, skirrets, salsify, common and sweet potatoes. Skirrets are no longer grown, but you can still find salsify in specialist greengrocers.

Part of the appeal of root vegetables is their inherent sweetness. In the seventeenth century, when only the rich could afford sugar, root vegetables tasted intensely sweet. The less sweet-flavoured ingredients you eat, the more sensitive you become to sweetness. At that time, many root vegetables were baked in elaborate pies or roasted in the embers of the fire and served with melted butter. Baked sweet and common potatoes were sauced with sack (a dry white wine) and sugar.

We've retained our love of roasted root vegetables, although modern taste dictates that they're served as a savoury dish. Usually, they're peeled, cut into chunks and tossed in olive oil with fresh herbs such as thyme or rosemary, although gratins are still popular. However, some chefs bake whole roots such as celeriac in a salt crust to bring out their natural sweet flavour.

By the eighteenth century, carrots were used in boiled puddings and still sometimes appear in Christmas pudding recipes. During the Second World War, the custom of using root vegetables in a wide variety of dishes was revived, no doubt in part due to the shortage of sugar. Today, root vegetables are added to sweet baked dishes for two reasons: firstly, they add moisture to the texture of a cake, pudding or bread; and secondly, they're widely regarded as making a dish more healthy.

POTATO BREAD

This is not a traditional British bread, but it fits well with our ever-expanding repertoire of dishes. It has an almost sourdough flavour and is delicious eaten with lots of butter. You need floury-textured potatoes for this recipe, such as Golden Wonder, King Edward or Maris Piper.

MAKES ONE FAMILY-SIZED LOAF

2 floury potatoes, peeled (about 400g/14oz)
1½ teaspoons fast-action dried yeast
370g/13oz strong white bread flour, plus extra
    for dusting

1½ teaspoons salt
70ml/2½ fl oz buttermilk

1 Cut the potatoes into large pieces. Place in a pan, cover with plenty of cold water, bring to the boil and cook briskly for 20 minutes or until soft. Drain the potatoes into a sieve, saving about 200ml/7fl oz of the cooking water. Leave the potatoes to steam dry for 5 minutes, then pass through a ricer, mouli or sieve.

2 Measure 100ml/3½ fl oz of the potato water into a small bowl and once it is tepid, sprinkle on the yeast and mix with a teaspoon. Leave for 5 minutes.

3 Put the flour in a large mixing bowl. Add 3 tablespoons of the flour to the yeasty water and leave for 15 minutes or until frothy. Meanwhile, mix the salt into the bowl of flour. Once the yeast is frothy, tip into the flour, add the mashed potato, buttermilk and about 100ml/3½ fl oz of the potato cooking water. Mix thoroughly until you have a soft, moist dough. The potato will make it become even more moist as you knead.

4 Turn out on to a clean work surface and knead for about 5 minutes or until the dough is smooth. The gloopy texture of the potato prevents it from being kneaded like a normal bread so throw it down and fold over as best you can. Place in a large clean bowl, cover with clingfilm, and leave for 1½–2 hours or until it has doubled in size.

5 Preheat the oven to fan 200°C/gas 7. Knock back the dough and lightly knead, then shape into a round loaf. Place on a well-floured baking sheet and lightly dust the top with flour. Invert a large bowl over the loaf and leave for 30 minutes or until puffy and risen.

6 Bake for 45 minutes or until golden and cooked. It should sound hollow when tapped on its bottom. Cool on a wire rack.

STEAMED CARROT PUDDING WITH CARDAMOM LEMON SYRUP

Carrots make wonderful moist puddings and cakes. Although cooks tend to think of steaming a pudding on a cooker hob, the oven is the easiest way to steam little puddings.

SERVES 5

55g/2oz sultanas
6 cardamom pods
115g/4oz butter, softened, plus extra for greasing
115g/4oz caster sugar
finely grated zest and juice of 2 lemons
2 medium eggs, lightly beaten
115g/4oz self-raising flour, sifted

55g/2oz fresh white breadcrumbs
2 carrots, peeled and finely grated

CARDAMOM SYRUP
10 cardamom pods
115g/4oz caster sugar
225ml/8fl oz water
finely pared zest and juice of 1 lemon

1 Make the cardamom syrup the night before you need it. Lightly bruise the cardamom pods and place in a small non-corrosive saucepan with the sugar and water. Add the finely pared lemon zest. Set over a medium heat until the sugar has dissolved, then simmer for 15 minutes. Leave until tepid, then add the lemon juice. Strain into a jug and pour 3 tablespoons of syrup over the sultanas for the pudding; cover and leave in a cool place. Cover and chill the remaining syrup.

2 When you're ready to cook your puddings, preheat the oven to fan 220°C/gas 8. Take five 150ml/5fl oz pudding basins. Using a basin bottom as a template, draw five circles on some baking parchment. Use the top of a basin to draw five more circles, then cut out all ten circles. Butter the basins and one side of each paper disc, then line the basin bottoms with small discs, butter-side up. Put in a deep roasting pan.

3 Strain the sultanas, adding their liquid to the rest of the syrup. Crush the 6 cardamom pods, remove the seeds, discard the pods and grind the seeds with a rolling pin or pestle and mortar.

4 In a large bowl, beat the butter and sugar with an electric whisk until pale and fluffy then beat in the crushed cardamom seeds, lemon zest and half the beaten egg. Fold half the flour into the butter mixture, followed by the remaining egg, breadcrumbs, lemon juice, carrots, sultanas and remaining flour. Spoon into the basins. Top with the larger paper discs, butter-side down, and cover each with a baggy square of foil tucked tightly around the rim. Pour boiling water into the roasting pan until it comes halfway up the sides of the basins. Cover the pan with a large sheet of foil and put in the oven. Cook for 1 hour.

5 Remove the puddings from the roasting pan and leave to rest for 10 minutes. Warm the syrup in a small non-corrosive pan over a low heat. The sponge will shrink back slightly, making it easy to turn out (remove the baking paper as you do so). Serve warm, with the syrup poured over.

CINNAMON PARSNIP CUPCAKES (GF)

The sweet, earthy taste of parsnips works well in cakes, in much the same way as carrots.
If you want to make ordinary cakes, just replace the gluten-free flour with plain flour.

MAKES 18 CUPCAKES

finely grated zest and juice of ½ lemon
finely grated zest and juice of ½ orange
115g/4oz parsnips, peeled and roughly grated
140g/5oz whole hazelnuts in their skins
30g/1oz gluten-free flour, sifted
1 teaspoon gluten-free baking powder
pinch of salt
1 teaspoon ground cinnamon
30g/1oz walnuts, roughly chopped
3 small eggs, separated
100g/3½ oz unrefined caster sugar

CREAM CHEESE ICING
55g/2oz full-fat cream cheese
100g/3½ oz icing sugar
30g/1oz butter, melted and tepid

DECORATION
20g/¾ oz hazelnuts, roughly sliced

1 Preheat the oven to fan 170°C/gas 4. Arrange 18 paper cupcake cases in two bun trays.

2 Put the lemon and orange zest in a large mixing bowl with ½ tablespoon of lemon juice and ½ tablespoon of orange juice. Set aside a further ½ tablespoon of each juice for the butter icing. Mix the grated parsnips into the citrus zest and juice. Set aside.

3 Put the hazelnuts and flour in a food processor and whiz in short bursts until the nuts are finely ground. Add the baking powder, salt and cinnamon, quickly whiz, then tip into a bowl and mix in the walnuts.

4 In a large, clean, dry bowl, whisk the egg whites until they form soft peaks. Add 2 tablespoons of unrefined caster sugar and continue to whisk, gradually adding the remaining sugar until it is all added and the egg whites form glossy, soft peaks.

5 Roughly beat the egg yolks. Using a metal spoon, fold them into the egg whites, then fold in one-third of the flour mixture, then one-third of the parsnips. Repeat until all the ingredients are mixed into the egg whites. Spoon into the paper cases, filling each one quite full. Bake for about 15 minutes or until the cakes spring back when lightly pressed.

6 Cool on a wire rack. Once cool, arrange in a small roasting pan, cover with foil, and chill for 2 hours. This firms up the cakes.

7 To make the cream cheese icing, beat together the cream cheese, icing sugar and remaining ½ teaspoon cinnamon using a wooden spoon. Add the reserved lemon and orange juice, then beat in the tepid butter. Spread a swirl of icing on each cake and chill until firm. Decorate with a few hazelnuts.

THE
ORCHARD

THE ORCHARD

There is something magical about an old orchard. Filled with billowing blossom and the buzz of insects in spring, it lures all who pass it to pause and dream of the warm days to come. In summer, the dappled, lichen-clad boughs of old apple trees are a pleasant place to lie under on a drowsy afternoon. In autumn, the orchard becomes a lively, social place as fruit is gathered from its ancient trees. Even in winter, edged silver with frost in the pale sunlight, it captures the imagination. A sleeping world that holds the promise of bounty.

Over the past fifty years, we've lost a sense of how abundant our orchards once were. There was a time when every county was filled with large and small orchards, and many a garden had at least one fruit tree. Apricots and greengages were trained along warm cottage walls. Cherry, damson and crab apple trees grew along the hedgerows and boundary walls. Quince and medlars could be found in old kitchen gardens. Aged fig, pear and apple trees thrived in city plots.

Today, a large number of our orchards have been grubbed up. According to Natural England, the government agency responsible for the protection and improvement of the natural environment, Wales lost 94 per cent of its commercial orchards between 1958 and 1992, while English commercial orchards have declined by 63 per cent since 1950.

The rise of cheap imported fruit has meant that only country cooks retain a sense of urgency when the fruit harvest gathers momentum in September. They feel the need to roll up their sleeves and process a seemingly endless supply of home-grown fruit before it falls to the ground to rot or be enjoyed by wasps. A neighbour's basket of figs will be exchanged for a bag of excess plums. Nothing must be wasted. The apple loft has to be swept and ordered, jam pans set to bubble, and the freezer filled with neatly labelled packets of lightly cooked greengages, plums, damsons and, for a lucky few, apricots.

Happily, fruit trees are enjoying a revival. Many old orchards are being restored and old local varieties replanted, such as the Tudor orchard at Lyveden New Bield in Northamptonshire. Some are being extended with local fruit varieties, for example on the Killerton Estate in Devon. Meanwhile, organisations such as Common Ground and the National Trust are busy encouraging both urban and rural communities to plant community orchards that can be tended and shared by all. Our renewed interest in self-sufficiency has led to allotments and suburban gardens being planted with small, easy-to-pick, modern varieties of fruit trees.

ABOVE LEFT Crab apples in the orchard at Sizergh
Castle, Cumbria.

ABOVE RIGHT Apples collected for cider making
in the orchard at Killerton, Devon.

In order to get the maximum pleasure from using up a glut of home-picked fruit, it is worth considering their baking qualities. With myriad pastry recipes to hand, there is no question that the textures and flavours of cherries, apricots, plums, apples and pears are wonderful encased in pastry. Look back over the centuries and you will find countless recipes for turnovers, pies, tarts and roly-polys, some flavoured with cinnamon, cloves or rose water, others kept plain and simple. A modern interpretation, the puff-pastry-based fine fruit tart, is just as good with apples or pears as it is with nectarines (see page 86).

Crumble and cobbler toppings appeared in the twentieth century, with countless permutations. The crumble topping, for example, can be varied by adding oats, ground hazelnuts or almonds. Fruit fillings can combine different fruits, for instance, strawberries or raspberries mixed with apple, or blueberries with pear.

If you want to expand your range of baked fruit recipes, start by thinking about the whole fruit. Quince, dessert apples, pears and plums are all transformed by being slowly baked in an aromatic syrup, flavoured with herbs such as rosemary or bay, or spices such as cinnamon, cloves or vanilla. All they need is a little cream as an accompaniment.

ABOVE LEFT Apples ready for harvest at Ardress House, County Armagh.

ABOVE RIGHT Pears growing in the orchard at Hardwick Hall, Derbyshire.

The next step is to imagine how the taste and texture of your chosen fruit might work if baked differently. The soft buttery texture of puréed cooked pears, for example, is superb baked as a custard. Add a hint of bitterness in the form of caramel, and you will enhance the pear flavour further – try a pear crème caramel (see page 61). The rich texture of puréed apricots baked in a custard benefits from a light fresh note, which can be created by adding some diced fresh apricot to the dish just before it goes in the oven (see page 189).

The succulent texture of apple and pear works well in cakes and muffins, while the juicy flesh of plums, apricots and cherries is better baked in a sugary batter that sops up their juice. There are endless possibilities to discover.

ABOVE LEFT Local varieties of apple tree blossom in the fruit orchard at Cotehele, Cornwall.

ABOVE RIGHT Ripening damsons at Hill House Farm on the Brockhampton Estate.

APRICOTS & CHERRIES

In late July, as summer deepens, the first English-grown cherries and apricots come into season. With their luscious texture and vibrant taste, both lend themselves perfectly to baking.

Cherries

In medieval times, cherries were as common as apples are today, albeit for a brief season. Their harvesting marked a period of general merrymaking, with cherry fairs across the country. Over the centuries, sweet, semi-sour and sour varieties of cherries were developed. The latter two were baked in pies, turnovers and batters. Their succulent texture also makes them well suited for muffins and cakes.

Cherries, however, release a lot of juice, which benefits from being lightly thickened. In *English Puddings, Sweet and Savoury* (1981), Mary Norwak recommends adding 2 tablespoons of tapioca flakes to 680g/1½ lb cherries (weight before stoning) to thicken the juices in her cherry pie. Alternatively, mix in a little arrowroot.

In a perfect world, I would recommend baking with semi-sour or sour cherries such as Kentish Knight and Kentish Morello respectively. Their superb flavour is amazing in dishes such as cherry batter pudding (see page 184). Sweet cherries can be used instead, but add a dash of lemon or orange juice to bring out their taste. Sadly, commercially produced sour culinary cherries have fallen out of favour in Britain. It is up to us to encourage their return.

Apricots

Although we may think of apricots as being an exotic import, they have been grown in English gardens from the mid-sixteenth century onwards. By the eighteenth century, no southerly wall was complete without a few apricot trees – hence the proliferation of recipes for 'green apricocks' (unripe apricots) at that time. Ripe or unripe, their delicately fibrous flesh ensures that, when cooked, they form a thick juice. Delicious when enriched with some butter, sugar and rose water, especially when baked in a pie. The texture of cooked apricots makes them well suited to all forms of pastry, pudding toppings and cream-based baked puddings.

CHERRY BATTER PUDDING

Sweet English cherries usually ripen in late July and early August. This is one of those simple traditional British puddings that is perfect for using up orchard fruit such as cherries or plums. The kirsch adds a subtle note. If you are lucky enough to have sour cherries, adjust the sugar to taste. You can, if you wish, make the batter an hour ahead, but cover and chill until needed.

SERVES 4

butter for greasing
450g/1lb cherries, halved and stoned
3 medium eggs
115g/4oz plain flour, sifted

70g/2½ oz caster sugar, plus 1 tablespoon
   for sprinkling
250ml/9fl oz full-fat milk
3 tablespoons kirsch

1 Preheat the oven to fan 190°C/gas 6. Liberally butter a 27cm/11in long shallow oval ovenproof dish.

2 Scatter the cherries over the base of the dish.

3 Break the eggs into a mixing bowl and, using a wooden spoon, gradually beat in the flour, followed by the sugar, so that it forms a smooth paste. Gradually beat in the milk and the kirsch, a little at a time, until you have a smooth, creamy batter.

4 Pour over the cherries and bake for 45 minutes or until the batter has puffed up and is crisp and golden. You may need to turn the dish halfway through baking to ensure that it cooks evenly. Remove and sprinkle with sugar. Serve hot, warm or at room temperature.

APRICOT ROSE WATER TURNOVERS

Fruit turnovers, as Mrs Beeton so wisely wrote in her *Book of Household Management* in 1861, are 'suitable for pic-nics'. They were once a popular hand-held pastry that every child loved. They can be made with raw or cooked fruit, or simply filled with jam.

MAKES 16 LITTLE TURNOVERS

250g/9oz fresh apricots, stoned and finely diced
55g/2oz caster sugar, plus 3 tablespoons for
    sprinkling

1 teaspoon distilled rose water
225g/8oz puff pastry, chilled (see page 84)
½ small egg white, beaten

1 Preheat the oven to fan 220°C/gas 8. Lightly oil two non-stick baking sheets. Place the diced apricots in a bowl with the sugar and rose water and mix thoroughly.

2 Roll out the pastry to about 5mm/¼ in thick and stamp out rounds using a 9cm/3½ in pastry cutter. Place the first pastry disc on the palm of your hand and spoon the sugared apricots on to one half of the pastry. Lightly brush the edge of one half with water, fold over the pastry and seal by pressing and crimping the edges together. As you make each turnover, place it on a lightly floured surface.

3 Re-roll the pastry trimmings and cut out more rounds, until you've used up all the filling. Liberally brush each turnover with beaten egg white, then liberally sprinkle with caster sugar. Arrange on their sides on the oiled baking sheets.

4 Bake for 25–30 minutes or until golden brown. Serve warm or at room temperature.

APRICOT CREAMS

These delicate-flavoured creamy puddings hide a little compote of apricots at the bottom. They're perfect for slightly unripe apricots.

SERVES 6 (PLUS ONE EXTRA FOR THE COOK!)

425g/15oz apricots, stoned
115g/4oz granulated sugar
1 vanilla pod, split

250ml/9fl oz double cream
5 medium eggs, beaten and strained

1 Preheat the oven to fan 180°C/gas 5. Lightly oil seven 150ml/5fl oz ramekin dishes or tea cups and place on some kitchen paper in a deep roasting pan.

2 Finely dice four apricots. Place in a small bowl and toss with 30g/1oz sugar. Divide between the ramekins or tea cups.

3 Roughly chop the remaining apricots. Place in a saucepan with 85g/3oz sugar and the vanilla pod. Set over a low heat until they start to release some juice, then increase the heat a little, cover and simmer for 20 minutes or until meltingly tender.

4 Remove the vanilla pod from the cooked apricots. Scrape the seeds into the fruit and rinse the pod. It can be dried and stored in a jar of sugar. Purée the apricots in a food processor. Once smooth, add the cream and eggs and whiz until thoroughly mixed.

5 Divide the mixture evenly between the ramekins or tea cups. Pour enough boiling water into the roasting pan to come halfway up the sides of the ramekins – or nearer three-quarters if using tea cups. Cover the pan with foil and bake for 35 minutes or until the creams are just set, with a slight wobble. Serve warm or at room temperature.

APPLES, PEARS & QUINCES

If the weather is fine, the first British apples are ripe for picking in early August. Pears soon follow, although the best appear in October, followed by quince in October or November. Together, they form the bedrock of British fruit puddings.

Apples

If there is one fruit that every home cook regularly contemplates, it is the apple. We have over two thousand different varieties in Britain, excluding cider apples. As Edward Bunyard wrote in *The Anatomy of Dessert* in 1933, 'No fruit is more to our English taste than the apple ... in a careful pomological study of my fellow-men I have met but one who really disliked apples, but as he was a Scotsman born in Bavaria, educated in England, domiciled in Italy, he is quite obviously ruled out.'

Over the centuries, we have developed three main groups of edible apples: cooking, dual-purpose and dessert. Many varieties of cooking apples were developed in the nineteenth century. A good cooker should be large, flavoursome and acidic and store well through the winter months. If it lacks acidity, its flesh will not cook into a fluffy pulp essential for melt-in-the-mouth pies, charlottes and soufflés. Bramley's Seedling remains the predominant commercially sold cooking apple, but some old orchards yield ultra-fluffy Golden Noble and Warner's King, or the once popular Howgate Wonder. In the north of England, you might happen upon Dumelow's Seedling or Keswick Codlin.

Dual-purpose apples tend to be eaten mainly as dessert apples, although they can be used as cooking apples early in the season when they're still sour. Charles Ross and James Grieve are classic examples. Naturally, dessert apples can also be baked: as they retain their shape, they tend to be favoured for recipes such as French apple tart.

Given a history of cooking apples that dates back to neolithic times, most British cooks will think nothing about baking stuffed apples or producing crumbles, sponge puddings and, of course, pies. The challenge lies in creating new and exciting flavour combinations. Apples taste wonderful cooked with berries, such as blackberries, strawberries, raspberries and blueberries. During the winter months, they also taste good with dried fruit, ranging from cranberries, blueberries and sour cherries to the familiar array of raisins, sultanas, currants and candied peel. Experiment with different flavourings: cinnamon, cloves and mixed spice are tried-and-tested partners for apples, but try fresh rosemary, lavender, distilled rose water, anise or honey.

Pears

English pears have fallen from favour when it comes to baking. Strange, when one considers that for centuries most pears were baked. In the fourteenth century, the wardon pear became famous for its quality in pies. Later any large baking pear that required keeping was called a 'wardon' or 'warden' as opposed to pear. Today, our supermarkets tend to sell three types of British-grown pears: Doyenne du Comice, Conference and Concorde, a cross between the former two varieties. All store well through the winter months and ripen into a juicy, sweet fruit.

The natural sweetness of pears means that if you want them to collapse into a fluff you need to add a little acidity to break down their flesh. Since they discolour quickly when cut, it's worth tossing the prepared fruit in a little lemon juice. This will also enhance their flavour. Apple brandy, Poire Williams (pear eau-de-vie) and kirsch all taste good with pears, as do rose water, various dessert wines and aromatic herbs such as rosemary and thyme. Cinnamon, cloves, star anise and ginger also work well in moderation. You can adapt many recipes to pears.

Quinces

Quince is magical ingredient that enhances the taste of apples and pears. Sadly, it has fallen into neglect, despite its exquisite fragrance and good storage life. It first became fashionable in the late thirteenth century when Edward I had numerous trees planted in his royal gardens. For the next five hundred years, it was widely grown in British orchards. We turned it's fruit into delicious pies and baked puddings, as well as jellies, sweetmeats, cheese (membrillo) and wine. F. A. Roach speculates in *Cultivated Fruits of Britain* (1985) that this decline was caused by the increasing popularity of soft fruit. Today, you're lucky if you see home-grown quinces sold by the roadside or in a farmers' market. Most are imported.

Store quinces in a cool place. If they're picked slightly green, ripen to a golden yellow in the kitchen. Rub off any grey fluff from their skin before cooking. They're too astringent to eat raw. If baking, you can cook quince unpeeled, sliced in half, either cored or not. Bake in a low oven with a lemon syrup flavoured with a vanilla pod, bay leaf or other spices such as cloves, cinnamon or star anise.

Quinces are quite tough to peel, quarter and core, but are worth the effort. Their flesh turns brown as you cut them, but don't worry, they'll turn a dusky rose colour as they cook. If you're combining quince flesh with apples or pears, it's sensible to pre-cook them slightly as they take longer to cook. They also taste delicious puréed (and sieved) in custard puddings. You can adapt the recipe for cinnamon pumpkin pie (see page 53) or apricot creams (see page 189).

APPLE AND BLUEBERRY MUFFINS

English blueberries come into season in August, so you can combine them with an early English dessert apple such as Discovery. Perfect for a late summer brunch. Muffins are best eaten on the day they're made.

MAKES 12 MUFFINS

115g/4oz butter
115g/4oz light muscovado sugar
150ml/5fl oz milk
2 medium eggs, beaten
1 dessert apple

250g/9oz self-raising flour
½ teaspoon bicarbonate of soda
1 teaspoon ground cinnamon
85g/3oz blueberries

1 Preheat the oven to fan 170°C/gas 4. Place 12 paper muffin cases in a muffin tray.

2 Melt the butter in a saucepan with the sugar. Cool slightly. Add the milk and then the eggs. Roughly grate the apple, skin and all (discard the core) and mix into the milk.

3 Sift the flour, bicarbonate of soda and cinnamon into a large mixing bowl. Mix thoroughly. Add the blueberries. Using a metal spoon, quickly fold in the apple and milk mixture, using as few strokes as possible. Do not over-mix.

4 Quickly spoon the mixture into the muffin cases and bake for 20–25 minutes or until cooked. Test by inserting a skewer: if it comes out clean, they're ready. Cool on a wire rack.

BLACKBERRY AND APPLE UPSIDE-DOWN CAKE

This National Trust recipe is perfect for tart dessert apples such as James Grieve or early Braeburns. It is equally good served warm as a pudding with clotted cream or as a cake at teatime.

SERVES 8

140g/5oz caster sugar, plus 1 tablespoon for dusting
140g/5oz butter, softened, plus 1 tablespoon
2 tablespoons pale muscovado sugar
3 dessert apples, peeled, cored and cut into quarters
250g/6oz blackberries

3 medium eggs, lightly beaten
200g/7oz self-raising flour, sifted
½ teaspoon ground cinnamon
2 tablespoons milk

1 Preheat the oven to fan 160°C/gas 3. Lightly oil a 23cm/9in spring-form cake tin. Line the base with baking parchment and lightly oil. Lightly coat the side of the tin by swirling 1 tablespoon caster sugar around the sides.

2 Melt a tablespoon of butter in a small pan, mix in the muscovado sugar and pour over the base of the tin. Arrange the apple quarters neatly around the bottom of the tin, along with a third of the blackberries.

3 In a large bowl, beat the remaining butter and caster sugar together until pale and fluffy, then gradually beat in the eggs, a little at a time. Fold in the flour and cinnamon, followed by the milk, so that the mixture forms a dropping consistency. Finally, fold in the rest of the blackberries.

4 Spoon the batter over the fruit in the tin. Bake for an hour or until the sponge is golden and springs back when lightly pressed. Check by inserting a skewer: if it comes out clean, the cake is cooked. Leave to cool in its tin on a wire rack for 5 minutes.

5 Run a knife around the side of the cake to loosen it, then invert the tin on to a serving plate and unclip and remove the tin. Peel off the paper. Serve hot, warm or at room temperature.

KILLERTON CIDER AND APPLE CAKE

In the old orchard on the National Trust's Killerton Estate in East Devon you will find at least 98 different varieties of apples. Many are unique to the West Country. Some are stored for eating and cooking, others are pressed to make cider. This cake, from Killerton House, also uses flour from Clyston Mill, the local working watermill, and cider from apples grown, harvested and pressed on the estate, using the 200-year-old cider press.

SERVES 8

55g/2oz sultanas
150ml/5fl oz dry cider
1 large cooking apple, peeled, cored and chopped
115g/4oz butter, softened
finely grated zest of 1 lemon
115g/4oz light muscovado sugar

2 medium eggs, lightly beaten
225g/8oz stoneground flour (white or wholemeal)
1 teaspoon baking powder
1 teaspoon ground cinnamon
1 tablespoon demerara sugar

1 Preheat the oven to fan 180°C/gas 5. Lightly oil and line a 20cm/8in cake tin. Put the sultanas in a medium bowl with the cider. Roughly dice the apples to the same size as the sultanas. Mix thoroughly in the cider.

2 In a large bowl cream together the butter, lemon zest and muscovado sugar until light and fluffy. Gradually beat in the eggs, a little at a time.

3 Sift the flour, baking powder and cinnamon into a bowl. Mix thoroughly, then gently fold the flour mixture into the creamed mixture, followed by the soaked fruit and cider. Gently mix until well incorporated, then spoon into the prepared tin.

4 Quickly sprinkle the demerara sugar over the top and bake for 45–60 minutes or until well risen and cooked through. Test by inserting a skewer into the centre of the cake: if it comes out clean, the cake is ready. Leave to cool in its tin on a wire rack for 5 minutes, then turn out and leave to cool.

APPLE AND CRANBERRY FLUTES

These are lovely at Christmas with the apple brandy cream. Filo is not an English pastry, but it's been assimilated into British cooking over the past 20 years. You need 12 sheets filo pastry, measuring about 30 x 38cm/12 x 15in, for this recipe. Most 250g/9oz packets contain 10 sheets.

SERVES 6

3 Bramley apples, peeled, cored and chopped
finely grated zest of 1 lemon
85g/3oz granulated sugar
115g/4oz dried cranberries
85g/3oz dried blueberries
12 sheets filo pastry (about 340g/12oz)

170g/6oz butter, melted and cooled
1 tablespoon icing sugar, for dusting

APPLE BRANDY CREAM
170ml/6fl oz double cream
1 tablespoon apple brandy or Calvados

1 Preheat the oven to fan 190°C/gas 6. Butter a large baking sheet.

2 Put the chopped apples in a saucepan with the lemon zest and sugar. Set over a low heat and stir occasionally until the apples start to release their juice. Simmer for 10 minutes or until the apples form a thick purée, then mix in the dried cranberries and blueberries. Leave to cool.

3 Unwrap the filo pastry, but keep it covered with a damp tea towel. Take one sheet of pastry and brush it with melted butter. Fold in half lengthways and brush with more butter. Place a thin line of the apple filling along one of the shorter edges – don't use too much or it will burst out when cooking. Fold the long side over the filling and roll it up in a cylindrical thin parcel, turn in the edges so that you seal each end of the filling as you go. Place on the baking sheet.

4 Repeat the process until you have 12 flutes on the baking sheet. Brush each flute with more butter, then cook for 20 minutes or until crisp and golden. Sift the icing sugar over them.

5 To make the apple brandy cream, put the cream and apple brandy in a large bowl and whisk until the cream forms soft peaks. Transfer to a pretty bowl and serve with the warm or cool apple flutes.

APPLE AND QUINCE CRUMBLE

When cooked together, quinces deepen the flavour of both apples and pears. They're delicious in this simple crumble, or you could top the mixture with a cobbler, pastry crust or sponge mixture.

If you'd like to make a nut crumble, you will need very hard butter. Freeze 55g/2oz diced butter, but take it out about 20 minutes before you need it, so that the butter is partially defrosted. Place 85g/3oz plain flour and 30g/1oz shelled almonds or hazelnuts in a food processor. Whiz until the nuts form fine crumbs. Add the semi-frozen butter and briefly process until the butter forms fine crumbs. Transfer to a bowl and mix in 30g/1oz sugar. Use as below.

SERVES 4

1 large quince
85g/3oz granulated sugar
2 large cooking apples, such as Bramley

CRUMBLE TOPPING
115g/4oz plain flour
55g/2oz very cold butter, diced
30g/1oz unrefined caster sugar

1 Preheat the oven to fan 180°C/gas 5. Peel, core and slice the quince. Place in a wide non-corrosive saucepan with 3 tablespoons water and the sugar. Set over a low heat and simmer for 10 minutes.

2 Peel, core and slice the apples. Add to the partly cooked quince and simmer for a further 10 minutes or until the apple is soft and fluffy and the quince is tender. Spoon the cooked fruit into a 27cm/11in long oval ovenproof dish.

3 Meanwhile, make the crumble topping. Put the flour and butter in a food processor. Whiz until the mixture forms fine crumbs, then tip into a bowl and mix in the sugar. Sprinkle over the fruit, using a fork to spread it out evenly. Don't press down, or it will become too compact. Cook for 30 minutes or until the topping is pale gold and looks cooked. Serve warm, with cream or custard.

APPLE AND BLACKBERRY MERINGUE

Soft-baked meringues make a gorgeous pudding in the early autumn, especially when topped with cider-poached fruit and apple brandy cream.

SERVES 6

6 medium egg whites
250g/9oz caster sugar
1½ tablespoons white wine vinegar
1½ teaspoons cornflour
icing sugar, sifted, for dusting

APPLE TOPPING
150ml/5fl oz dry cider
85g/3oz unrefined caster sugar

4 strips finely pared lemon zest
4 dessert apples, such as Cox's Orange Pippin
    or Braeburn
250g/9oz blackberries

APPLE BRANDY CREAM
285ml/10fl oz double cream
4 tablespoons apple brandy or Calvados

1 Preheat the oven to fan 140°C/gas 2. Line a baking sheet with baking parchment. In a large, dry bowl, whisk the egg whites until they form stiff peaks, then gradually whisk in the caster sugar until the mixture is thick and glossy. Using a flat metal spoon, fold in the vinegar and cornflour. Spread the mixture evenly over the baking parchment in a 20 x 30cm/8 x 12in rectangle. Bake for 20 minutes or until soft and marshmallow-like.

2 Leave to rest on the baking sheet for a few minutes. Liberally dust a sheet of baking parchment with icing sugar. Gently tip the meringue on to the sugar-dusted parchment, peel away the baking paper and leave to cool.

3 To make the apple topping, put the cider, sugar and lemon zest in a non-corrosive saucepan. Set the pan over a low heat until the sugar has dissolved and simmer

gently while you peel, core and dice or slice the apples. Add these to the cider syrup and simmer gently for 4 minutes or until just tender. Mix in the blackberries, return to a simmer, then remove from the heat. Using a slotted spoon, transfer the fruit to a bowl. Simmer the syrup for a few minutes until it thickens slightly, remove the lemon zest and pour over the fruit. Leave until cold.

4 To make the apple brandy cream, put the cream and apple brandy in a large bowl and whisk until the cream forms soft peaks. Chill until needed.

5 To serve, cut the meringue into six squares and place one on each serving plate. Top with some of the apple brandy cream, then spoon on the fruit so that it spills over the meringue.

APPLE BREAD

This unusual recipe from the National Trust makes a moist, slightly sour bread that keeps well. It's particularly good eaten with cheese.

MAKES A 450G/1LB LOAF

185g/6½ oz peeled, cored and chopped
    Bramley apples
2 scant teaspoons fast-action dried yeast
225g/8oz strong white flour

225g/8oz stoneground wholemeal flour, plus extra
    for dusting
1 teaspoon salt
40g/1½ oz dried apples, chopped

1 Put the apples in a saucepan with 2 tablespoons of water. Cover and cook gently over a low heat for about 10 minutes or until the apples have collapsed into a pulp. Using a wooden spoon beat until smooth, then set aside until cool.

2 Measure 100ml lukewarm water into a small bowl. Sprinkle the yeast over the water and mix lightly. Leave for 10 minutes or until the yeast has dissolved and looks frothy.

3 Meanwhile, mix the flours and salt together in a large bowl. Mix in the chopped dried apples. Add the apple purée and liquid yeast to the flour and mix until you have a soft dough. You may need to add a little more water. Turn out on to a clean surface and knead for 10 minutes or until the dough is smooth and silky.

4 Place the dough in a large bowl and cover with clingfilm. Leave in a warm, draught-free place for 1½ hours or until it has almost doubled in size.

5 Turn the dough on to a clean surface and lightly knead before shaping into a round loaf. Dust with wholemeal flour and place on a greased baking sheet. Invert a large bowl over it and leave for about 30 minutes or until it is one and half times its original size. Preheat the oven to fan 200°C/gas 7.

6 Lightly cut a cross in the centre of the loaf and place in the oven. Bake for 40–45 minutes or until it looks cooked and sounds hollow when tapped on the bottom. Leave to cool on a wire rack.

ROAST PEARS WITH ROSEMARY

Baking is a lovely way to serve autumn fruit. Quinces and pears are particularly good and can be served warm or at room temperature. Instead of rosemary, you can flavour the fruit with vanilla, cinnamon or cloves.

SERVES 6

300ml/10½ fl oz dessert wine such as Sauternes
55g/2oz caster sugar
30g/1oz butter, roughly diced

6 sprigs rosemary
12 small ripe pears

1 Preheat the oven to fan 200°C/gas 7. Put the Sauternes, sugar, butter and rosemary in a wide flameproof casserole dish. Peel and halve the pears. As you prepare each pear, slip it into the wine, coating it thoroughly to prevent it from discolouring.

2 Set over a high heat and bring to the boil, then place the uncovered dish in the oven. Bake for 45–50 minutes, until the pears are tender and caramelised in some places. Serve with the warm buttery juices and lots of double cream.

CARDAMOM PEAR TART TATIN

This is one of my favourite puddings. I first wrote it for *Modern British Food* in 1995, but it was my husband who had the inspired idea of combining cardamom with the buttery pear. It's irresistible, especially when accompanied by an apple and Calvados ice cream, in which case this recipe will stretch to four people. You need an 18cm/7in cast-iron omelette pan – it must have an ovenproof handle – for this recipe.

SERVES 2–4, DEPENDING ON GREED

225g/8oz puff pastry (see page 84)
6 green cardamom pods
55g/2oz granulated sugar
30g/1oz butter, softened

2 tablespoons Poire Williams (pear eau-de-vie, optional)
1 tablespoon lemon juice
6 ripe pears

1 Preheat the oven to fan 220°C/gas 8. Roll out the pastry on a lightly floured surface. Then, using a plate that is slightly larger than your pan as a template, cut out a circle of pastry about 3mm/⅛ in thick. Lightly prick with a fork, and chill while you prepare the remaining ingredients.

2 Lightly crush the cardamom pods so that you can remove the black seeds. Discard the green husks, and then, using either a pestle and mortar or a rolling pin, roughly crush the seeds. Mix half of them with the sugar and set the remaining half aside. Using your fingers, press the butter on to the base of your pan to it coat it evenly. Sprinkle the sugar over the butter and set aside.

3 Place the Poire Williams and lemon juice in a mixing bowl. If you are not using any alcohol, add a little extra lemon juice to prevent the fruit from discolouring. Peel one pear at a time, cutting it into quarters and removing the seeds and tough core. Thoroughly coat in the lemon juice and then repeat with the remaining fruit.

4 Tightly pack the pears in a circle in the frying pan, pressing their rounded sides lightly into the sugar. Fill the centre with the roundest pear and then place over a medium-high heat. The pears will shrink slightly as they release their juices, so do not be afraid to add another slice or two as they cook. Stand over the pan at this stage, moving it around slightly if one area is browning faster than another.

5 As soon as the sugar has caramelised, scatter with the remaining cardamom seeds and remove from the heat. Quickly press the pastry circle on to the pears, tucking the edges down the side of the pan.

6 Bake for 25 minutes or until the pastry is a beautiful golden colour and well risen. Do not worry if some of the caramelised juices bubble out. Remove from the oven and leave to rest for 5 minutes.

7 To turn out, put a slightly larger plate upside down over the pan and, holding it in place, invert the pan, giving a good shake. The tart should slip out, juices and all. Serve hot with lots of thick double cream.

ICED QUINCE AND PEAR PIE

In the seventeenth century, tarts and pies were works of art. The 1685 edition of Robert May's *The Accomplisht Cook* includes elaborate designs for pie crusts for everything from quince pies to gooseberry tarts. You can make this pie as simple or as ornate as you wish.

SERVES 6

shortcrust pastry (see page 80) made with
    40g/12oz flour and 170g/6oz butter
juice of ½ lemon
1 tablespoon apple brandy or Calvados
pinch of ground cinnamon
pinch of ground ginger
tiny pinch of ground cloves
30g/1oz caster sugar

1 quince
6 pears
milk for brushing

ROSE WATER ICING
70g/2½oz icing sugar
½ tablespoon distilled rose water
½ tablespoon lemon juice

1 Line a baking sheet with baking parchment, and place a 20cm/8in tart ring on the parchment. Cut the pastry in half. Roll out half of the pastry and line the tart ring. Trim the excess from the edges and chill.

2 Roll out the remaining pastry and cut out a 23cm/9in circle. Gently transfer on to a sheet of greaseproof paper. Take a further sheet of greaseproof paper and draw a 23cm/9in circle – this is going to be your stencil. Draw the design that you wish to cut from your pie crust, such as a fleur-de-lis. Place the paper on top of your sheet of pastry and using a cocktail stick, prick the design into the pastry. Remove the paper and cut out the design. Chill for 1 hour.

3 Put the lemon juice, apple brandy, spices and caster sugar in a non-corrosive saucepan. Peel, quarter, core and roughly dice the quince. Add to the lemon juice mixture. Set over a medium heat and simmer gently for 10–15 minutes.

4 While the quince is cooking, peel, quarter, core and roughly dice the pears. Add to the simmering quince and cook for a further 10 minutes or until the fruit is tender but still holding its shape. Drain the fruit in a sieve, collecting the juice. Put the fruit in a bowl.

5 Return the juice to the pan and boil briskly until it forms a thick syrup. Add to the fruit and leave to cool.

6 Preheat the oven to fan 190°C/gas 6. Fill the pastry-lined tart ring with the cooked fruit, discarding any excess syrup. Lightly brush the edge of the tart ring with milk, then gently place the lid over the fruit and, using a teaspoon, press down to seal the edges. Trim the excess pastry and brush the lid with milk. Bake for 50 minutes or until golden and crisp. Once cooked, gently slide the pie off its paper on to a wire rack, remove the ring and leave to cool.

7 Once cold, sift the icing sugar into a small bowl. Using a wooden spoon, stir in the rose water and lemon juice to make a smooth icing, then ice the pastry lid.

CHOCOLATE PEAR CAKE (GF)

This National Trust recipe can be served as a pudding or for tea. Be sure to choose juicy ripe pears for the best flavour and don't overcook the sponge so that it retains a gooey centre. This cake is particularly good accompanied by crème fraîche.

SERVES 8

85g/3oz unrefined caster sugar, plus extra for
    dusting
85g/3oz shelled hazelnuts in their skins
85g/3oz dark chocolate, broken into chunks

85g/3oz butter, diced
3 medium eggs, separated
4 ripe pears, peeled, cored and halved
1 tablespoon icing sugar

1 Preheat the oven to fan 180°C/gas 5. Lightly grease a 20cm/8in spring-form cake tin. Line the base with baking parchment. Lightly grease the parchment and dust the tin with a heaped tablespoon of caster sugar.

2 Spread the hazelnuts on a baking sheet. Roast in the oven for 10 minutes or until they smell really nutty. Tip the nuts into a clean tea towel and rub off the brown skins. Once cold, place the nuts in a food processor. Whiz in short bursts until they're finely ground. Do not over process or they'll form a paste. Set aside.

3 Put the chocolate and butter in a small bowl over a pan of just-boiled water off the heat. Stir occasionally until melted, then remove the bowl from the pan and leave to cool slightly.

4 In a large bowl, whisk together the egg yolks and caster sugar until they're pale and thick. Fold the egg yolks and ground hazelnuts into the cooled melted chocolate.

5 Whisk the egg whites with a clean dry whisk in a clean dry bowl until they form soft peaks. Stir a quarter of the whites into the chocolate mixture to loosen it, then gently fold in the remaining whites. Spoon into the prepared tin, level the surface and arrange the pears, cut side down, on top of the mixture.

6 Bake for 40 minutes, until the pears are soft and cake is cooked through. Leave to cool in the tin for 5 minutes, then remove and leave to cool on a wire rack. Dust with icing sugar before serving.

PLUMS & GREENGAGES

The British plum or 'gage', as some varieties are called, is a fruit apart. Unlike the bland, firm-fleshed Asian varieties that are imported all year round, it has a short season that stretches from around the third week of July until mid-September. Each British plum variety is in season for a week or two, and then it is gone for another year. There are many varieties, some purely regional, such as the Pershore or yellow egg plum, and the small Cornish Kea plum. Both were bred as culinary varieties. Such rare plum varieties are now being submitted for special classification within the European Union to help protect and promote them.

To the uninitiated, British plums might look a little dull, but toss some halved, purple-fleshed, green-skinned Avalons or blushing pink and yellow Marjorie Seedlings in sugar and bake under a buttery puff pastry crust and you will understand their appeal. Once cooked, their sweetness is transformed into an intensely rich, fruity, sweet-sour taste that demands plenty of accompanying cream or custard. Tender-fleshed greengages collapse into a sweet froth that tastes delicious topped with an almond sponge or crumble, while intensely flavoured Victoria plums invite a hint of star anise or cinnamon and a yeast-risen pastry base to soak up their juice.

If you want to intensify the plum flavour of your baked dish, add a hint of wild plum in the form of sloes, bullaces or their close relation, damsons. All make excellent preserves, which can be used as a flavouring, whether it be gin, jelly or syrup.

It is well worth cooking and freezing batches of British plums while they're in season. There are few things as warming as a plum pudding in the depths of winter.

PLUM AND DAMSON COBBLER

Small, dusky damsons add an incredible depth of flavour to any plum dish. They normally appear at the beginning of August and can often be found in farmers' markets. It only takes a few moments to stone them and the results are well worth the effort. Beware, however, that you don't get their juice on your clothes – it was once used as a dye and it will stain. This filling is also good in buttery pies and baked sponge puddings.

SERVES 6

800g/1¾ lb plums, halved and stoned
200g/7oz damsons, halved and stoned
115g/4oz granulated sugar, or to taste

COBBLER TOPPING
225g/8oz self-raising flour
pinch of salt

85g/3oz cold butter, diced
50g/1¾ oz caster sugar
1 medium egg
about 4 tablespoons milk, plus extra for brushing
2–3 tablespoons granulated sugar

1 Preheat the oven to fan 170°C/gas 4. Mix the plums and damsons with the granulated sugar in a bowl; add more sugar if you have a sweet tooth. Tip into a 20 x 20cm/8 x 8in china baking dish, 5cm/2in deep. You can also bake this recipe in a 1.8kg/4lb pie dish as seen in the photograph opposite. Place in the oven while you prepare the topping.

2 In a food processor, whiz the flour, salt and butter until it forms fine crumbs. Tip into a mixing bowl. Stir in the caster sugar. Break the egg into a measuring jug, beat well and add enough milk to reach a scant 150ml/5fl oz. Pour into the flour mixture and roughly mix into a very wet dough, using your hand.

3 Transfer to a liberally floured surface and lightly knead into a rollable dough. Remove the plum dish from the oven. Roll out the dough to 1cm/½ in thick. Stamp out scones, using a 6cm/2½ in diameter pastry cutter. As you cut the scones, arrange them on top of the fruit so that they barely overlap and there are gaps in between the scones. Lightly knead together the trimmings and re-roll and stamp out more scones, until the dish is covered. Pour a scant tablespoon milk into your eggy measuring jug, brush over the scones and liberally sprinkle with granulated sugar.

4 Immediately place the cobbler in the oven. Bake for 40 minutes or until golden and oozing with sugary juices. Serve warm, with clotted cream.

PLUM OR GREENGAGE SOUFFLÉ

Plums, greengages, sour cherries and apricots all make wonderful soufflés. This is not a classic egg- based or white sauce-enriched soufflé, rather it depends on a stabilised thickened fruit purée. You can prepare the fruit purée in advance, and then add the whisked egg whites immediately before you are ready to bake. The purée should be tepid or cold before you fold in your whipped egg whites, otherwise they'll collapse.

SERVES 6

400g/14oz greengages or plums, halved and stoned
140g/5oz caster sugar
3 tablespoons Mirabelle eau-de-vie or kirsch
2 tablespoons arrowroot

butter, softened, for greasing
6 medium egg whites
icing sugar for dusting

1 Place the fruit in a non-corrosive saucepan with 115g/4oz of the caster sugar and 2 tablespoons of Mirabelle or kirsch. Cover and bring to the boil, stirring occasionally, and then simmer uncovered for 15 minutes or until soft. Purée the cooked fruit and return to the pan.

2 In a small bowl, mix together the arrowroot and 1 tablespoon Mirabelle or kirsch. Mix in a spoonful or two of the hot fruit purée, then return it to the pan of puréed fruit. Set over a medium heat and stir regularly for about a minute, or until it comes to the boil and thickens. Tip into a bowl and leave to cool.

3 Remove the top rack from the oven. Preheat the oven to fan 200°C/gas 7. Butter a 1.5 litre/2½ pint soufflé dish and place in a small, deep roasting pan. You can also divide this mixture into smaller soufflé dishes (see photograph). Prepare in the same way but cook for 10–15 minutes depending on the size of your dishes.

4 Whisk the egg whites until they form soft peaks, add 30g/1oz caster sugar and continue to whisk until stiff. Stir two large spoonfuls of whisked egg white into the fruit purée to loosen the mixture, then fold in the remainder with a metal spoon, gently scooping the heavier purée from the bottom of the bowl up over the egg whites until they're lightly integrated.

5 Spoon into the soufflé dish, smooth the top and place in the roasting pan. Pour in enough boiling water to come one-quarter of the way up the side of the dish. Bake for 20–25 minutes or until a skewer comes out almost clean. Remove from the oven, dust with icing sugar and serve immediately.

FELBRIGG HALL FRUIT TART

This comes from a handwritten twentieth-century recipe found at the National Trust's Felbrigg Hall in Norfolk. It uses a pint of fruit – in other words, you fill a measuring jug up to the 565ml/1 pint mark – regardless of whether it's stoned cherries or chopped apples. For plums, this works out as about 450g/1lb chopped fruit. You then sweeten your chosen fruit with sugar and cover with a self-raising shortcrust pastry, which bakes into a soft pastry.

SERVES 4

450g/1lb stoned and chopped plums or greengages
1 tablespoon water
85g/3oz granulated sugar, or to taste

PASTRY
170g/6oz plain flour
½ teaspoon baking powder
pinch of salt
85g/3oz cold butter or lard, diced

1 Preheat the oven to fan 200°C/gas 7. Put the fruit, water and sugar to taste in a 565ml/1 pint capacity pie dish.

2 To make the pastry, sift the flour, baking powder and salt into a mixing bowl. Mix thoroughly. Rub in the butter or lard with your fingertips until it resembles fine crumbs. Add a little cold water and mix to make a stiff paste.

3 Turn the pastry on to a floured surface and roll out to the same shape as the pie dish but a good 2.5cm/1in larger. Cut 1cm/½ in wide strips from the edges of the pastry: you will need enough to go round the rim of the pie dish. Wet the rim of the dish, line with the strips of pastry and then dampen the strips. To cover the pie, lightly roll the pastry around the rolling pin, lift and unroll over the dish. Press down along the edges with a teaspoon or fork before trimming using a small sharp knife. Cut two or three tiny holes in the raw crust with a knife and place in the oven. Bake for about 25 minutes, or until the crust is golden and crisp. Serve hot, warm or cold with lots of cream.

THE
HEDGEROW

THE HEDGEROW

Beyond the kitchen door lies a world that still shapes the imagination of British cooks. Hedgerows filled with blackberries, elderberries and damsons. Ditches lush with wild garlic and sorrel. Meadows peppered with field mushrooms. Even town dwellers succumb to this vision, and seek out elderflowers, nettles and brambles in neglected corners of their cities.

In recent years, the idea of foraging for food has become increasingly popular, yet the reality is that wild ingredients have always formed a part of our culinary heritage. Their importance within our diet has waxed and waned with the changing fashions and economic circumstances of the country.

In medieval times, delicacies such as cowslips, violets and wild strawberries were as much a part of a gentleman's cook's ingredients as dittander, good King Henry and meadowsweet. The latter three declined in popularity as cultivated horseradish replaced dittander, spinach ousted good King Henry, and beer became more popular than mead infused with meadowsweet.

Most old recipe books were written for the gentlewoman of the house. They mainly focused on how to preserve, distil or make dainty sweetmeats, including wild foods. In 1609, for example, Sir Hugh Plat included numerous receipts for preserving cowslips,

damsons, hazelnuts, broom buds, violets and walnuts in his *Delightes for Ladies*. By 1685, Robert May's *The Accomplisht Cook* has recipes for barberry and damson tarts, along with candied violets, cowslips, primroses and suchlike for salads.

By the eighteenth century, cookbooks had become increasingly general in their subject matter, but the recipes for wild food remained focused on preserves. In *The Compleat Housewife* (1758) by Eliza Smith, for instance, there are recipes for elder, birch and cowslip wine, along with conserve of hips, pickled barberries and pickled broom buds.

This is not to say that cooks didn't prepare wild foods in other ways, just that it was not considered necessary to publish a recipe. A daughter would learn from her mother how to cook a bilberry pie or turn damsons into damson cheese, a dense preserve of fruit. Recipes for blackberries appear in the nineteenth century in the context of helping the poor. In the 1853 edition of *Modern Domestic Cookery*, based on the work of Mrs Rundell, the editor wrote under an entry for blackberry jam: 'In families where there are many children there is no preparation of fruit so wholesome, so cheap, and so much admired, as this homely conserve.'

ABOVE LEFT Hedgerow lines a footpath in the grounds of Sissinghurst Castle Garden, Kent.

ABOVE RIGHT Bramble leaves and berries ripening in the autumn sun.

Rationing during the Second World War provoked another revival of interest in food from the hedgerow. In 1942, B. James, writing in *Wild Fruits, Berries, Nuts and Flowers: 101 Good Recipes for Using Them*, says 'In England up to fifty years ago the delicious wild fruits and flowers of the countryside, as well as the vegetables of the sea, were always used and greatly prized. In their place today factory-made foods, synthetic flavourings, vinegars and essences are bought in tins and bottles ... It has taken a World War to make us realise just what we have lost of the good things of byegone days.' He includes some baking recipes such as elderberry pie, blackberry and apple curd for filling tarts, and sweet-briar (rose hip) tart. A second movement towards self-sufficiency and 'the good life' occurred in the early 1970s. In 1972, Richard Mabey's book *Food for Free* launched an alternative approach to the environment, which has led to a greater desire to protect and nurture the countryside.

Today, serving wild foods in restaurants is seen as an expression of culinary identity that is directly linked to the landscape. However, many chefs employ 'sci-fi' techniques and the food you might eat in their restaurants bears little resemblance to the dishes you

ABOVE LEFT A hedgerow bursting with cow parsley and other wild flowers.

ABOVE RIGHT Wild garlic grows alongside bluebells and campion at Antony, Cornwall.

might cook at home. It is only when we begin to integrate more wild foods into domestic cooking that a true sense of modern British cooking will emerge.

If you are interested in foraging, it is important to read up on the subject and, if possible, get extra guidance until you are experienced. Richard Mabey's *Food for Free* is still in print, or look up Roger Phillips, Miles Irving and Antonio Carluccio in the bibliography (page 316), as they too have written excellent books.

Baking is a good way of extending hedgerow foods, whether it's using wild mushrooms on a pizza or turning damsons, elderberries and rose hips into preserves that can be used in cakes and scones.

ABOVE LEFT Cowslips, a popular preserve in the seventeenth century, in flower on Box Hill, Surrey.

ABOVE RIGHT Chanterelle mushroom (*Cantharellus cibarius*).

WILD HERBS
& FLOWERS

Every year, the sight of the first primroses and sweet violets on a mossy bank fills me with delight. Spring has arrived. The ditches are lush with clumps of wild garlic (ramsoms) and the woods will soon be speckled white with flowering wood sorrel. Countless pleasures lie ahead. Walks down dappled lanes scented by the frothy white heads of sweet cicely and elderflowers, and picnics on the chalk downs carpeted with wild thyme and marjoram. So many delicacies to be gathered and enjoyed.

From a baker's perspective, such foods should be handled with the lightest of touches. Most do not respond to the dry heat of an oven, so it's a question of subtly introducing them to a baked product after cooking (see also pages 130–133). This can be done in a number of ways.

In savoury dishes, you can flavour a butter or infuse an oil that is then added to the baked dish, for example wild garlic butter melted into crusty bread (see page 226) or wild thyme-infused olive oil, drizzled over a pizza just before you take it to the table.

Sweet dishes can be flavoured by infusing herbs or flowers into a sugar syrup that is then poured over the baked dish, or by beating the freshly chopped herb into cream or an icing for a cake, meringue or pastry. An almond cake is wonderful drenched in a homemade elderflower syrup (see page 229). However, take care to gently wash anything you pick.

As a guiding principle, ask yourself why you're using a particular wild ingredient. What does it bring to a dish? What does it suggest to the eater? Are you trying to capture a sense of the season or landscape? If so, are you effective in your choice? The muscat scent of elderflowers will suggest summer to most Britons, but will an eater be aware of the difference in flavour between wild and cultivated thyme?

WILD GARLIC BREAD

In March, wild garlic runs rampant in damp ditches and shady woods. By April, its beautiful white flowers often speckle bluebell woods and it's hard to resist picking a sprig or two to take home. This bread is particularly good with tomato salad, especially if you scatter the salad with garlic flowers.

SERVES 4–6

small handful wild garlic leaves
85g/3oz butter, softened
2 tablespoons finely chopped parsley

salt and freshly ground black pepper
1 baguette

1 Preheat the oven to fan 190°C/gas 6. Wash and dry your wild garlic leaves, then finely chop. You will need about 1 tablespoon – but adjust the quantity to taste as wild garlic leaves become increasingly strong as the summer progresses.

2 Beat together the butter, wild garlic leaves and chopped parsley. Season to taste. Using a serrated knife, cut the bread diagonally as though you were slicing it, but do not cut all the way through the loaf: you want to create buttered slices that are still attached at the base.

3 Liberally spread the wild garlic butter on both sides of each 'slice'. Wrap the loaf in foil. When you're nearly ready to serve, bake for 10–15 minutes or until the butter has melted and the bread is piping hot.

BAKED EGGS WITH WILD SORREL

Common sorrel (*Rumex acetosa*) is one of the first plants to appear in spring. It's best picked early in the season, before it flowers. It has a refreshing 'sharp' flavour, similar to cultivated sorrel (which you can also use), as it contains oxalic acid. This is poisonous if eaten in very large quantities – something that is hard to do given its astringent taste. This recipe can be served as a starter or eaten as a light lunch or supper, with crusty, buttered bread.

SERVES 2

butter for greasing
1 small bunch of sorrel
115ml/4fl oz single cream

salt and freshly ground black pepper
2 medium eggs

1 Preheat the oven to fan 180°C/gas 5. Lightly butter two ramekin dishes.

2 Wash the sorrel leaves and remove the stalks by taking each leaf, folding it in half so that the stalk forms one edge, and pulling the stalk away from the leaf. Finely shred the leaves, using a sharp knife.

3 Measure 6 tablespoons cream into a small pan. Bring to the boil. Add the sorrel and allow to wilt for about a minute. Lightly season, then divide the mixture between the two ramekins and leave to cool.

4 Break an egg on top of the sorrel mixture in each ramekin. Spoon 1 tablespoon of the remaining cream over each egg and season lightly.

5 Put the ramekins into a small roasting pan and pour in enough boiling water to come halfway up the sides of the dishes. Bake for 10–12 minutes or until the egg white is set and the yolk still runny. Serve immediately.

STICKY ELDERFLOWER SYRUP CAKE

Elders flower in June or July, depending on where they grow. Their frothy white flowers add an amazing muscat flavour to syrups and taste wonderful with almonds. This can be served as a cake or a pudding. Accompany the latter with a few fresh strawberries, tossed in elderflower syrup or liqueur. If you can't find the elderflower liqueur, use a muscat grape white dessert wine.

SERVES 6

170g/6oz butter, softened
170g/6oz caster sugar
finely grated zest of 1 lemon
3 large eggs, separated
85g/3oz self-raising flour, sifted
85ml/3fl oz St-Germain elderflower liqueur
85g/3oz ground almonds

ELDERFLOWER SYRUP
finely pared zest and juice of 1 lemon
1 elderflower head, washed
30g/1oz granulated sugar
100ml/3½ fl oz water
3 tablespoons gin

1 Preheat the oven to fan 170°C/gas 4. Oil a 20cm/8in spring-form cake tin. Line the base with baking parchment.

2 Beat the butter and caster sugar together until pale and fluffy. Add the lemon zest, then gradually beat in the egg yolks, followed by 2 tablespoons of flour and the elderflower liqueur. Lightly fold in half the almonds, followed by half the remaining flour. Then fold in the remaining almonds and the rest of the flour.

3 Immediately whisk the egg whites in a clean, dry bowl until they form firm peaks. Gently fold them into the cake mixture, then spoon the mixture into the cake tin and bake for 50 minutes or until cooked. Test by inserting a skewer into the centre of the cake: if it comes out clean, the cake is cooked. Turn out and remove the paper. Place the hot cake on a wire rack over a deep-rimmed plate.

4 While the cake is baking, make the elderflower syrup. Put the pared lemon zest in a small non-corrosive saucepan with the elderflower head, sugar and water. Set over a low heat until the sugar has dissolved, then simmer gently for 10 minutes. Cover, remove from the heat, and leave to infuse.

5 As soon as you have turned the cake out of its tin, return the syrup to the heat and bring to the boil. Add the lemon juice and gin and strain into a jug. Prick the warm cake with a fork and then, using a spoon, drip-feed the syrup into the cake in small batches. Make sure it is evenly fed and use all the syrup. Leave until cold before serving.

RHUBARB AND ELDERFLOWER CHARLOTTE

Elderflowers add a fragrant sweetness to sour fruits such as gooseberries and rhubarb. You can add them to all manner of baked puddings, such as this updated easy charlotte. A classic baked charlotte is where a mould is lined with buttered sliced bread, filled with fruit, topped with more bread, and then baked until crisp and golden. It is then turned out.

SERVES 6

1.1kg/2lb 7oz rhubarb, trimmed
3 elderflower heads
55g/2oz butter, plus extra for buttering

115g/4oz granulated sugar, plus 1 tablespoon
6 medium slices good white bread

1 Preheat the oven to fan 180°C/gas 5. Trim the rhubarb and cut into 2.5cm/1in lengths. Dip the elderflower heads into a bowl of cool water, shake off the excess water, and strip the tiny flowers from their green stems. Discard the stems.

2 Melt 55g/2oz butter in a wide, non-corrosive saucepan over a low heat. Add the rhubarb, elderflowers and 115g/4oz sugar. Mix thoroughly and stir occasionally until the rhubarb begins to soften and release some juice. Sweeten to taste if necessary, then tip into a 20 x 30cm/8 x 12in oval baking dish.

3 Liberally butter the bread on both sides, then cut off the crusts. Cut each slice into four triangles. Arrange over the fruit in overlapping rows and press down so that the bread can soak up some of the juice as the rhubarb cooks. Sprinkle the bread with 1 tablespoon sugar. Bake for 35–40 minutes or until the bread is golden and crisp and the fruit is bubbling and soft. Serve warm or at room temperature.

WILD MUSHROOMS

From the first morels emerging in spring to the late autumn blewits, black trumpets and hedgehog fungus, there is a plentiful supply of British wild mushrooms to be enjoyed. However, novices wishing to forage for fungi should ensure that an expert checks their finds, as mistakenly eating a poisonous mushroom can be fatal. Luckily, it's becoming easier to buy a wide variety of native wild mushrooms, ranging from chanterelles to the delicious but expensive cep, or penny bun as it used to be called in Britain.

All are excellent baked and taste particularly good mixed with cream in tarts and pies. Mace, nutmeg and cayenne pepper enhance their flavour, as do lemon zest, thyme, parsley and tarragon.

The art of a good cook lies in balancing the taste, texture and aroma of a dish. Since the one characteristic that all mushrooms share is their somewhat slippery texture when cooked, it is important to counterbalance this when baking. The contrast of a crisp pie topping or a flaky vol-au-vent case, for example, makes a creamy fricassee of mushrooms utterly alluring. Encasing sautéed mushrooms within the crust of a calzone (see page 239) has a similar effect. Alternatively, you can emphasise the succulent flesh of a field mushroom by baking it with a crumbly contrasting topping (see page 237).

CHANTERELLE TART

As soon as the weather turns warm and damp in the summer, chanterelles (*Cantharellus cibarius*) emerge on mossy ground in deciduous woods. Look out for them in farmers' markets and good greengrocers or delis. You can, of course, make this recipe with button mushrooms instead. If serving as a starter, accompany with a little leafy salad.

SERVES 4–6

225g/8oz shortcrust pastry (see page 80)
3 tablespoons cold-pressed rapeseed oil
4 slices back bacon, trimmed and diced
1 onion, finely diced
250g/9oz chanterelles, trimmed and wiped

salt and freshly ground black pepper
1 medium egg
1 medium egg yolk
200ml/7fl oz double cream
20g/¾ oz Wensleydale cheese, finely grated

1 Preheat the oven to fan 180°C/gas 5. Roll out the pastry on a lightly floured surface and line a 23cm/9in tart tin. Prick the base of the pastry, line with greaseproof paper, and fill with baking beans. Chill for 30 minutes.

2 Bake the pastry case for 15 minutes. Once cool enough to handle, remove the beans and paper.

3 Set a frying pan over a medium heat. Add the oil and, once hot, fry the bacon briskly for 5 minutes or until lightly coloured. Add the onion, reduce the heat, and fry for 10 minutes or until soft. Roughly tear the trimmed mushrooms and stir into the bacon mixture. Increase the heat slightly and cook briskly for 5 minutes or until the mushrooms are lightly cooked and any excess liquid has evaporated. Remove from the heat and season to taste.

4 Beat together the egg, yolk and cream. Mix in the fried mushrooms and adjust the seasoning to taste. Tip into the pastry case, sprinkle with the cheese, and immediately return to the oven. Bake for 30 minutes or until golden and slightly risen. Serve hot, warm or cold.

STUFFED MUSHROOMS

Field mushrooms or large flat mushrooms are incredibly rich stuffed. These can be served as a vegetarian starter. Accompany with a pretty mixed leaf salad.

SERVES 4

85g/3oz butter
2 shallots, finely diced
8 flat mushrooms
55g/2oz button mushrooms, trimmed
115g/4oz soft white breadcrumbs

finely grated zest of 1 lemon
1 small bunch of parsley, leaves finely chopped
2 medium egg yolks
salt and freshly ground black pepper
pinch of cayenne pepper

1 Preheat the oven to fan 180°C/gas 5. Using some of the 85g/3oz butter, liberally butter a non-stick roasting pan, which should be large enough to hold the mushrooms in one layer.

2 Set a small non-stick frying pan over a medium-low heat. Add the remaining butter and, once melted, stir in the shallots and cook for 8 minutes or until soft and golden.

3 Meanwhile, peel the flat mushrooms; remove the stalks and set aside. Place the mushrooms in the buttered roasting pan. Finely chop the stalks. Wipe clean the button mushrooms and finely chop. Stir into the softened shallots and cook briskly for 5 minutes or until soft.

4 Tip the buttery mushroom mixture into a mixing bowl. Add the breadcrumbs, lemon zest, chopped parsley and egg yolks. Mix together and season to taste with the salt, black and cayenne pepper.

5 Pile the filling into the flat mushrooms and bake for 25 minutes or until the mushrooms are just tender and the topping flecked gold.

FIELD MUSHROOM CALZONE

Throughout the summer months, meadow mushrooms were traditionally fried or pickled by British cooks. Today, they are also eaten in a wide range of baked dishes, from pies and vol-au-vents to tarts, turnovers and pizzas. Calzone is, quite simply, a pizza turnover. Don't make the filling too wet or the pizza dough will turn soggy.

Field mushrooms can be gathered from early summer until autumn. They love warm, damp weather and rich pasture land. However, if gathering them yourself, use a good guidebook, as there are some poisonous lookalikes such as the Yellow Stainer (*Agaricus xanthodermus*).

SERVES 2

½ quantity pizza dough (see page 112)
200g/7oz buffalo mozzarella
3 tablespoons extra virgin olive oil, plus extra
    to serve
1 clove garlic, finely chopped
1 teaspoon dried chilli flakes (optional)

225g/8oz field mushrooms, trimmed, peeled and
    cut into 1cm/½ in cubes
salt and freshly ground black pepper
½ tablespoon lemon thyme leaves
3 tablespoons finely grated Parmesan

1 Place a heavy baking sheet in the centre of your cold oven. Preheat the oven to fan 230°C/gas 9. Drain the mozzarella and pat dry. Cut into 1cm/½ in cubes and place in a colander. Gently press to release some of the excess moisture.

2 Set a non-stick frying pan over a medium-high heat. Add the olive oil, then the garlic and chilli, if using. As soon as it begins to sizzle, add the diced mushrooms. Season and stir-fry briskly for 3 minutes or until they have released most of their liquid. Mix in the lemon thyme and tip into a bowl. Once cool, mix in the finely grated Parmesan.

3 Roll out your pizza dough as described on page 112 into two discs about 20cm/8in in diameter. Spread the mushrooms over half of each disc of dough, taking care not to cover the raised edge. Scatter the mozzarella cubes over the mushrooms. Fold the uncovered half of the dough over the filling. Pinch the edges firmly together so that no juices can escape. Bake on the hot baking sheet for 10 minutes or until the calzone have puffed up and turned crisp and golden. Brush with a little olive oil before serving.

HEDGEROW FRUITS

The perfect hedgerow yields juicy sweet blackberries, elderberries, rose hips, haws, sloes and hazelnuts each autumn. In an idyllic world, this hedge would also contain the odd crab apple tree or be interspersed with an old cherry or damson tree. Once, such hedgerows were common, but in the 1950s around half our ancient hedges were ripped up in favour of a more industrialised system of agriculture. Today, they're starting to be replanted as their intrinsic value in protecting nature is beginning to be recognised.

When such hedges were commonplace, rural cooks would gather their fruit and transform it into pies, jellies, syrups, wines and vinegars. The intense flavour and high nutritional content of such fruit formed an essential part of the rural diet.

During the Second World War, books such as *Wild Fruits of Britain* (1939) by Jason Hill revived the practice of foraging. Mr Hill stresses the benefits of using hedgerow fruits as a flavouring by turning them into preserves. This is sensible, since many have an intense flavour.

An entire pie filled only with elderberries, delicious as they are, might be overwhelming unless you love strong, slightly tannic, port-like flavours. Better to mix them with other fruit, such as plums and blackberries.

It seems to me that while modern tastes will happily use blackberries in a wide variety of dishes, more intensely flavoured wild fruits are regarded more cautiously. Sloes, crab apples and elderberries can all be turned into delicious preserves such as jellies, jams and firm fruit cheeses. Crab apple or elderberry jelly, for example, taste wonderful spread on a sponge cake or oat scone (see page 102), while a spoonful or two of sloe jelly adds an incredible depth of flavour to a plum pie. I've included one example, but recipes for homemade jams and jellies are not hard to find. Such preserves will give your baked dishes a uniquely British flavour.

For more blackberry recipes, see blackberry and apple upside-down cake (page 196), apple and blackberry meringue (page 201) and hazelnut and blackberry roulade (page 248).

DAMSON ROLY-POLY

Roly-polys were once a popular country dish as they are very filling and keep out the damp cold in winter. They're easy to make and you can use another jam, such as plum or strawberry, instead of damson. The breadcrumbs create a lighter pastry.

SERVES 4–6

200g/7oz damson jam
200g/7oz self-raising flour
pinch of salt
30g/1oz soft white breadcrumbs

70g/2½ oz shredded beef or vegetarian suet
30g/1oz caster sugar
1–2 tablespoons milk
1–2 tablespoons granulated sugar

1 Preheat the oven to fan 200°C/gas 7. Liberally grease a shallow baking tin (this will catch the juices if it leaks). Put the jam in a small saucepan and set over a very low heat. You need it just warm enough to spread easily.

2 Put the flour, salt, breadcrumbs and suet in a food processor and whiz to fine crumbs. Add the caster sugar, briefly process, and tip into a mixing bowl. Stir in about 150ml/5fl oz cold water. The dough should have a soft, light, spongy texture.

3 Tip on to a floured surface, squish into a soft rectangle and roll out into a rectangle about 1cm/½ in thick. Don't make it too thin – you don't want any holes. Thickly spread with the warm jam, leaving a 2.5cm/1in margin around the edges. Brush the edges with water, then gently roll up the pastry from the long side and firmly seal all the edges together before sliding it on to the baking tin. If it's not tightly sealed, the juices will leak out and caramelise on the tin.

4 Brush the roly-poly with milk and liberally sprinkle with granulated sugar. Bake for 20–25 minutes until golden brown and puffy. Serve warm, with custard.

ELDERBERRY JELLY

Elderberry jelly has a gorgeous, almost port-like flavour. It can be added to baked fruit puddings, spread on cakes or served as an accompaniment to oat scones (see page 102). Elderberries ripen from August to October. Pick when inky black. Remember that the jelly needs to drip overnight. The yield of fruit jellies varies depending on how juicy the fruit is; however, as a rough guide, for every 450g/1lb sugar added, a yield of about 700g/1lb 9oz will result.

1.8kg/4lb ripe elderberries
150ml/5fl oz water

granulated sugar (see step 2)
juice of 2 lemons

1 Dip the elderberry heads into plenty of cold water and shake gently to dislodge any insects. Drain and pull the berries off their stems and place in a saucepan with the water. Crush thoroughly to release plenty of juice. Bring to the boil, cover and simmer for about 15 minutes or until tender.

2 Pour into a jelly bag with a large bowl placed underneath and leave to drip overnight. Do not squeeze the jelly bag or the jelly will be cloudy. Discard the pulp from the jelly bag. Measure the strained juice. You will need 450g/1lb sugar to every 565ml/1 pint elderberry juice.

3 Sterilise your jam jars by washing them in hot soapy water, rinsing in very hot water, and then placing them in a cool oven (fan 130°C/gas 1) to dry. Alternatively, wash in the dishwasher then leave to dry with the dishwasher door partially open.

4 Put the elderberry juice, lemon juice and sugar in a preserving pan or saucepan with a sugar thermometer clipped on to the side. If you don't have a thermometer, chill a saucer in the fridge. Heat gently, stirring occasionally, until the sugar has dissolved, then increase the heat and quickly bring to the boil. Boil vigorously, stirring regularly to prevent the jelly from catching, until it reaches setting point (106°C/220°F) on the thermometer or until a drop of jelly on the cold saucer wrinkles slightly when pushed with your fingertip.

5 Immediately remove from the heat and leave to cool slightly. Skim off any scum and pour into the sterilised jam jars. Cover with a disc of waxed paper, wax side down, carefully clean the rim with a clean damp cloth, then tightly cover with damp cellophane discs. These will contract as they dry, forming an airtight covering when the jelly is cool. Label, date and store in a dark cool place.

ALMOND BLACKBERRY CAKE

Few can resist this luscious almond cake after an afternoon picking blackberries. Serve warm with clotted cream for tea or pudding.

SERVES 6

115g/4oz butter, softened
115g/4oz caster sugar, plus 2 tablespoons for
  sprinkling
3 medium eggs, lightly beaten
1 teaspoon almond extract

40g/1½ oz self-raising flour
100g/3½ oz ground almonds
1 tablespoon milk
340g/12oz blackberries

1 Preheat the oven to fan 180°C/gas 5. Lightly oil a 20cm/8in non-stick spring-form cake tin. Line the base with baking parchment. Lightly oil.

2 Place the butter and sugar in a large mixing bowl and beat until pale and fluffy. Gradually beat in the eggs, a little at a time, followed by the almond extract. Beat in the flour, followed by the ground almonds. Finally stir in the milk and spoon into the buttered cake tin. Lightly level the surface.

3 Gently press the blackberries into the top and liberally sprinkle with 2 tablespoons sugar. Immediately place in the centre of the oven and bake for 30 minutes or until a skewer inserted into the centre comes out clean.

4 Leave the cake in the cake tin for 3–4 minutes before carefully removing from the tin. Serve warm or at room temperature, with clotted cream.

HAZELNUTS
& WALNUTS

Hazelnuts (*Corylus avellana*), also known as cob nuts, are indigenous to Britain and were commonly collected from woods and coppices. However, by the sixteenth century, new varieties, including filberts (*Corylus maxima*), had been introduced. Both have been cultivated commercially in Kent ever since. Many new varieties were developed in the nineteenth century, the most famous of which became known as the Kentish Cob, although in reality it's a filbert. You can easily find wild hazelnut trees, but they're hard to harvest as the nuts need to be ripe and brown, and grey squirrels tend to get there first.

It is not known when walnut trees were first introduced into Britain, although the nuts have certainly been eaten here since Roman times. By the sixteenth century, they were planted both in open country and in orchards. They were grown primarily for their wood as their ability to crop was badly affected by their susceptibility to our spring frosts. Nevertheless, home-grown walnuts were much appreciated, primarily to be eaten after dinner.

Today, you can still find walnut trees growing in parkland, especially in the southern counties of England. Many of the nuts fall while they're still green. These can made into pickled walnuts. The second harvest comes when the nuts within the green pithy fruit have turned brown – the nuts will need to be carefully dried if they are not to turn mouldy.

Both hazelnuts and walnuts lend themselves to baking. They have a high oil content, so store in a cool, dark place, otherwise they can turn rancid. Both are delicious added to breads, cakes and tarts. Hazelnuts, like almonds, can be used instead of flour in cakes and puddings. For further recipes, turn to the index.

HAZELNUT AND BLACKBERRY ROULADE

This simple flourless roulade tastes of warm autumn days. Roasting the hazelnuts allows you to remove their slightly bitter brown skin, but it also deepens their nutty flavour. Serve as a pudding or as a teatime cake.

SERVES 8

HAZELNUT ROULADE
100g/3½ oz shelled hazelnuts in their skins
5 medium eggs, separated
100g/3½ oz caster sugar, plus extra for dusting

BLACKBERRY FILLING
285ml/10fl oz double cream
3 tablespoons icing sugar, plus extra for dusting
250g/9oz blackberries

1 Preheat the oven to fan 180°C/gas 5. Cut a piece of baking parchment slightly larger than a 27 x 38cm/ 11 x 15in baking tin. Lightly oil the baking sheet. Fold each edge of the baking parchment so that it forms a 2.5cm/1in rim. Snip each corner so that it stands up above the baking tin. Press the paper into the tin, secure with metal paper clips, and lightly oil.

2 Spread the hazelnuts on a baking sheet and roast for 10 minutes, until they release a nutty aroma. Tip into a clean tea towel. Rub vigorously to remove their papery brown skins. Place the nuts in a food processor and leave to cool, then whiz in short bursts until they're finely ground.

3 Set aside 2 tablespoons caster sugar from the 100g/3½ oz sugar. Whisk the remaining sugar with the egg yolks until they form a thick, pale mousse that leaves a trail on the surface when you lift the whisk.

4 In a separate bowl, using a clean, dry whisk, whisk the egg whites until they form soft peaks. Add the reserved 2 tablespoons caster sugar and whisk until thick and slightly glossy. Quickly fold the ground hazelnuts into the egg yolk mousse, followed by the whisked egg whites. Pour into the prepared tin, spread evenly, and bake for 12 minutes or until just done. It should be springy and shrinking away from the edges. Leave to cool on a wire rack. Discard the paper clips.

5 Once the roulade is cool enough to handle, put a clean tea towel on a work surface. Place a large sheet of greaseproof paper on top. Sprinkle the paper with caster sugar and invert the roulade on to it. Carefully peel away the baking paper. Trim the edges of the roulade and leave until cold.

6 To make the filling, put the cream in a large bowl. Sift in the icing sugar and whisk until it forms soft peaks. Fold in the blackberries and spread over the roulade, leaving a 2cm/¾ in border all around. Use the paper to roll up the roulade from the short end. Ease on to a serving plate, dust with icing sugar, and serve.

HAZELNUT AND RAISIN BREAD

This makes a gorgeous bread which freezes well. Use unblanched hazelnuts, they'll add a lovely nutty flavour to this fragrant fruited bread. It's delicious with butter and honey for breakfast or tea.

MAKES ONE 450G/1LB LOAF

55g/2oz shelled hazelnuts, cut in half
55g/2oz raisins
1 teaspoon fast-action dried yeast
250g/9oz organic strong white flour
½ teaspoon salt

¼ teaspoon ground cinnamon
1 medium egg
½ tablespoon runny honey
½ tablespoon hazelnut or walnut oil

1 Mix the hazelnuts with the raisins. Set aside. Measure 3 tablespoons tepid water into a small bowl, sprinkle the yeast over the water. Gently mix and leave for 10 minutes or until it has dissolved, smells of fresh yeast and looks frothy.

2 Sift the flour, salt and cinnamon into a large bowl. Break the egg into a measuring jug, beat with a fork, then add the honey and enough water to make 150ml/5fl oz liquid in total. Tip into the flour and knead for 10 minutes or until it forms a soft, silky dough.

3 Turn out the dough on to a work surface, flatten out the dough, and press in half the hazelnuts and raisins. Roll up and knead, and then repeat the process until the fruit and nuts are evenly distributed throughout the dough.

4 Pour the oil into a large clean bowl. Add the dough, turning it to coat lightly in the oil. Cover with clingfilm and leave in a warm, draught-free place for about 2 hours or until it has doubled in size.

5 Turn out the dough and knock back by lightly kneading. Shape it into a torpedo-shaped loaf and place on an oiled baking sheet. Cover with a large inverted bowl. Leave in a warm, draught-free place for 45 minutes, or until it has doubled in size. Preheat the oven to fan 220°C/gas 8.

6 Bake for 15–20 minutes or until it has a golden crust and sounds hollow when tapped on the bottom. Remove and leave to cool on a wire rack.

HAZELNUT BRITTLE CHEESECAKE

This classic National Trust cheesecake recipe is served topped with ultra-sweet, nutty hazelnut brittle, but you could serve the cheesecake plain or with some sugared blackberries. The brittle is made by caramelising the hazelnuts in sugar and then smashing them into 'brittle' pieces.

SERVES 10

200g/7oz digestive biscuits
55g/2oz butter, melted
600g/1lb 1oz full-fat cream cheese
150g/5½ oz caster sugar
2 medium eggs
1 scant teaspoon vanilla extract
15g/½ oz cornflour

finely grated zest and juice of 1 lemon
170ml/6fl oz double cream

HAZELNUT BRITTLE
115g/4oz granulated sugar
115g/4oz blanched hazelnuts

1 Preheat the oven to fan 170°C/gas 4. Lightly oil a 25cm/10in spring-form cake tin. Line the base with baking parchment and lightly oil.

2 Put the digestive biscuits in a plastic bag and crush with a rolling pin until they form fine crumbs. Tip into a bowl and mix in the melted butter. Gently press the mixture evenly over the bottom of the lined tin. Bake for 10 minutes, then remove from the oven and reduce the oven temperature to fan 140°C/gas 2.

3 Beat together the cream cheese and caster sugar until smooth. Using a wooden spoon, mix in the eggs, vanilla, cornflour, lemon zest and juice until smooth. Take care not to over-beat. Finally, stir in the cream.

4 Pour the mixture over the biscuit base and bake for 45 minutes or until lightly coloured and cooked through so that it has a slight wobble in the centre. Leave to cool in the tin on a wire rack. Once cold, slide a knife around the edge of the cheesecake to loosen it, then unclip the tin and gently slide the cake off its baking paper. Loosely cover with clingfilm and chill in the fridge for a couple of hours until cold.

5 To make the hazelnut brittle, lightly oil a non-stick baking sheet. Put the granulated sugar in a heavy-bottomed saucepan with 150ml/5fl oz cold water and set over a low heat for about 10 minutes or until the sugar has dissolved, then add the nuts. Cook gently until the sugar starts to caramelise and turns golden brown. As it starts to colour, swirl the nuts around in the pan to prevent them from catching. Do not let it get too dark or it will taste bitter. Immediately pour on to the oiled baking sheet and leave to cool. Once cold, place in a plastic bag and, using a rolling pin, smash into small chunks. Scatter over the cheesecake before serving.

SOFT HAZELNUT MACAROONS

These chewy hazelnut macaroons are perfect for serving with a raspberry ice cream or at teatime. Prepare them in the morning of the day before you want to eat them, as they need time to dry out. They keep well in an airtight container for a couple of days.

MAKES 28 BISCUITS

150g/5½ oz ground or whole shelled hazelnuts
1 large egg white
115g/4oz caster sugar

few drops of vanilla extract
icing sugar, for dusting

1 Line a baking sheet with greaseproof paper. If you can't buy ground hazelnuts, finely grind the whole hazelnuts in short bursts in a food processor (until a similar consistency to shop-bought ground almonds).

2 Whisk the egg white in a clean, dry bowl until it forms stiff peaks, then gradually whisk in the caster sugar, a little at a time, until the mixture is glossy. Mix in the ground hazelnuts and vanilla.

3 Dust your hands in lots of icing sugar and roll out a grape-sized ball of hazelnut meringue between the palms of your hands. Gently flatten and lay out on the baking sheet. Dust your hands with more icing sugar and repeat the process until all the mixture is used. Leave to dry out for a minimum of 8 hours or overnight.

4 Preheat the oven to fan 140°C/gas 2. Bake the biscuits for 10 minutes or until they are pale and slightly cracked. Using a palette knife, transfer them to a wire rack. Dust with icing sugar and leave until cold.

WALNUT CAKE

This is a dry-textured sweet cake with a satisfyingly nutty flavour, reminiscent of Fuller's walnut cake you used to be able to buy. Delicious with a cup of tea, but only for those with a sweet tooth.

SERVES 8

WALNUT CAKE
85g/3oz walnut kernels, plus 8 walnut halves
  for decoration
170g/6oz butter, softened
170g/6oz caster sugar
3 medium eggs, beaten
170g/6oz self-raising flour, sifted

BUTTER CREAM
115g/4oz butter, softened
85g/3oz icing sugar, sifted
1 teaspoon vanilla extract

BOILED ICING
285g/10oz caster sugar
1¼ teaspoons glucose syrup
2 medium egg whites
few drops of vanilla extract

1 Preheat the oven to fan 170°C/gas 4. Lightly oil two 20cm/8in sandwich tins. Line the base of each with baking parchment. Lightly oil.

2 To make the walnut cake, roughly chop 85g/3oz walnuts using a sharp knife, and saving all their crumbs. They should be smaller than the chopped walnuts you can buy.

3 In a large bowl, beat the butter and caster sugar together until pale and fluffy, then gradually beat in the first two eggs. Fold in a tablespoon of flour, then beat in the last egg. Tip in the flour and walnuts and lightly fold into the butter mixture. Divide evenly between the two sandwich tins and smooth over the surface.

4 Bake for 20 minutes or until the sponge springs back when lightly pressed and a skewer inserted into the centre of the cake comes out clean. Leave to cool in the tin on a wire rack for 10 minutes. Turn out and peel off the baking paper. Leave until cold.

5 To make the butter cream, beat the butter until pale and fluffy, then beat in the icing sugar and a few drops of vanilla extract, to taste. Once the cakes are cold, sandwich them together with the butter cream.

6 To make the boiled icing, put the sugar in a saucepan, add 150ml/5fl oz water and clip a sugar thermometer on to the side of the pan. Set over a low heat until the sugar has dissolved. Add the glucose syrup. Bring to the boil and, when it gets very close to 116°C/240°F, start whisking the egg whites to stiff peaks using an electric whisk. As soon as the syrup reaches 116°C/240°F, continue to whisk as you pour a thin stream of syrup into the whisked egg whites. The mixture will billow up into a thick, opaque meringue and then collapse down again slightly. Whisk in the vanilla, and after a couple of minutes pour the icing over the cake. Don't leave too long as it thickens as it cools. Using a wet palette knife, smooth the icing over the cake. Decorate with the walnut halves. Leave for 2 hours or until the icing is firm.

CHOCOLATE AND WALNUT BROWNIES

Everyone loves chocolate brownies. They might be an American import, but they've become part of the British baking repertoire and an essential cake on the summer fête stall. Make mini-brownies by cutting them into smaller squares. You can use halved hazelnuts instead of walnuts.

SERVES 12

200g/7oz dark chocolate, chopped
2 large eggs, beaten
1 large egg yolk
225g/8oz light muscovado sugar
2 teaspoons vanilla extract

85g/3oz plain flour, sifted
pinch of salt
100g/3½ oz walnut halves
140g/5oz butter, diced

1 Preheat the oven to fan 180°C/gas 5. Lightly oil a 18 x 27cm/7 x 11in tin or a 20cm/8in square tin and line with baking parchment.

2 Put the chocolate in a large bowl that will neatly fit over a pan of just-boiled water (off the heat). You may need to replace the boiling water to allow the chocolate to melt.

3 In a separate bowl, roughly beat together the eggs, egg yolk, sugar and vanilla. In another bowl, measure out the sifted flour, salt and walnuts.

4 Add the butter to the melted chocolate and stir until it has melted. Remove the bowl from over the water. The chocolate mixture should be warm, rather than hot, by now.

5 Quickly beat the egg mixture into the chocolate. As soon as they are evenly mixed, stir in the flour mixture and pour into the prepared tin.

6 Bake for about 20 minutes for the rectangular tin or 25 minutes for the deeper square tin. You need to keep a keen eye on it, as you're looking for a gooey brownie and it will continue to cook in the tin once removed from the oven. The cake crust should be lighter brown than the centre. If you insert a skewer into the centre, moist crumbs should cling to it. You don't want the brownie to be too wet or too dry. Leave to cool in the tin on a wire rack. When ready to serve, cut into 12 pieces.

THE
LARDER

THE LARDER

Few people now remember the pleasure of stepping into an old-fashioned larder. It belongs to an era before central heating and refrigeration became widespread. Cool and shady, it was a quiet place filled with alluring smells and hidden goodies. Its north-facing windows were covered with a fine fly mesh. Its thick, airy shelves were always laden with a mixture of fresh and dried foods, from whole cheeses and cold hams to packets of sugar and canisters of tea.

The larder was the domain of the cook, off-limits to children craving a spoonful of jam and adults intent upon an illicit late-night snack. Not that that stopped anybody. For the cook, stepping in from the bustle and heat of the kitchen, it allowed time to think while surveying its contents. Inspiration could be found amongst the jars of spices, sugar and preserved fruit, especially when combined with a quick survey of the leftovers such as stale bread and sponge cake. For the raider, there were biscuits to be filched from tins and illicit chunks of cake or cold pudding to be broken off and munched. A place to experiment with unexpected taste combinations.

The name 'larder' dates back to its medieval origins and the Anglo-Norman word *lard* meaning bacon. It originally referred to a place to store bacon. All but the humblest homes needed somewhere cool to hang their sides of home-cured bacon through the

winter months. Many houses also used the larder to salt the meat and preserve fish and vegetables. In large houses, there would be separate rooms for storing other foods. The buttery or butlery was for storing alcohol, from the French *bouteillerie* for bottle store; and the pantry for looking after the bread and tableware, from the French *paneterie*, meaning breadstore. These two rooms would be combined into one in smaller houses.

In Elizabethan times, most large houses had two larders, one 'wet' and one 'dry'. The wet larder was for storing raw, salted and pickled fish and meat. The dry larder was used for storing flour, bread, spices, sugar, rice, salt, herbs, preserves and suchlike. Some foods were suspended from the ceiling in nets, baskets and sacks, others placed in tubs, pots and barrels. Valuable spices and cones of sugar were often locked up in special cabinets. Only the cook and housekeeper would have the key.

By Georgian times, many large houses had specialised larders for game and pastry (the pantry), alongside their wet and dry larders. Potted dishes were kept and made in the wet larder, while the pantry could also be used for making pastries. The dry larder began to house new foods, from pickles and chutneys to tea, coffee and chocolate.

ABOVE LEFT The dry larder at Lanhydrock, Cornwall, used for storing dry foodstuffs.

ABOVE RIGHT Cupboards in the dry larder at Lanhydrock, storing spices, preserves and tins.

In the latter part of the nineteenth century, the larder as we know it began to emerge. Estates began to be less self-sufficient and more dependent on shop-bought foods. Less was preserved for the year, echoing the practice of urban homes, where tins, bottles and packets were stored in the larder or dresser, alongside cheese, pies and cakes. The large houses still kept their cool wet larders for fish and meat. By the 1850s, many even had ice-chests or boxes, the precursor of the refrigerator.

Today, the kitchen cupboard and fridge have replaced the larder in most homes. Nevertheless, a well-stocked kitchen cupboard can be a great source of inspiration. Nutmeg could be used to flavour a custard tart or cheesecake, or a spinach soufflé. The scent of tea might create a yen for a spiced fruit brack. When stuck for ideas, it's worth rummaging around your kitchen cupboards to see what suggests itself. But don't be annoyed if you discover that someone has got there before you and eaten the sponge cake you were saving for a trifle. They too are following a long and ancient tradition.

RIGHT Spice cabinet in the Housekeeper's Room at Tredegar House, Newport, South Wales.

SUGAR & SPICE

Sugar and spice are as essential to bakers as butter and eggs. Every kitchen cupboard should contain an array, carefully chosen to suit its owner's taste. Since I have a weakness for gingerbread, fruit cakes and sticky toffee puddings, I always have dark and light muscovado sugars, tins of treacle and golden syrup, and jars of powdered ginger, cinnamon and mixed spice.

Sugar

If you're new to baking, it's helpful to understand what different sugars bring to baked recipes. Sugar (sucrose) comes from two main sources: sugar cane and sugar beet.

Sugar cane is the source for unrefined brown sugars. These taste less sweet and increasingly bitter (in a nice minerally way) the darker and less refined they are. The darkest is molasses sugar, followed by dark muscovado, light muscovado and the more granular demerara sugar. In baking terms, these are all quite heavy sugars and add a moist texture and depth of flavour to baked recipes.

Always check that these brown, less refined sugars are soft when you buy them. They become dry and hard in storage. To keep them soft, place a chunk of bread into a clean container, then empty your newly purchased packet of sugar on to the bread and seal the container. This keeps the sugar soft and crumbly. The bread will dry out and become rock hard.

You can also buy unrefined golden granulated, caster and icing sugar. Refined granulated, caster and icing sugar can be made from either sugar cane or sugar beet.

Many baking recipes advocate using unrefined golden caster sugar and icing sugar. I have to admit that I prefer the pure taste of refined sugar in many of my recipes. The unrefined sugars have a slightly caramelised flavour, which is suitable for some recipes, such as cinnamon parsnip cupcakes (see page 174), but not for more delicate items, such as almond rose fairy cakes (see page 137).

Molasses, black treacle and golden syrup are all by-products of refining cane sugar. Molasses is not widely available to the domestic cook. It is the darkest and least sweet of all three substances. Black treacle is sweeter and contains 65 per cent sugar, along with a large amount of calcium, iron and potassium. It is made by blending, evaporating and filtering a proportion of the bitter molasses with other, sweeter, sugar syrups, all of which are released at a later stage in the refining process. Both molasses and black treacle can be added to malt breads, fruit cakes, gingerbreads and parkins to add a rich, sticky moistness.

Golden syrup is also made from some of the excess refining syrups. However, unlike black treacle and molasses, it is subjected to its own refining process, which gives it a clear golden colour and pleasing flavour. It contains about 80 per cent sugar, so is usually combined with sugar in a baking recipe such as flapjacks or treacle tart.

Spices

Choosing spices is part of the fun of baking. There are always new flavour combinations to discover and your selection of spices should be a source of inspiration whenever you open your cupboard. Try to mentally match up your main chosen baking ingredient with different spices.

To keep them at their best, you should store spices in airtight containers in a cool, dark, dry place. Some spices quickly lose their aroma. Ground mace and ginger, for example, have a very short shelf life. Others, particularly whole spices such as cloves or star anise, keep their fragrance for years. If you don't bake often, it is worth checking your spices once in a while. Simply sniff them. If the ginger has lost its heat, or the ground cinnamon smells slightly soapy, they're probably past their best.

When using spices, remember that less is more. Spice adds a subtle nuance to a dish; it should never be overpowering. The aim of the baker is to make a cake, bun or biscuit taste wonderful and leave the eater intrigued as to why it tastes so amazing.

ICED SPICED BISCUITS

Be warned, these biscuits are very addictive – iced or un-iced. They keep well in a tin, if you can resist eating them.

MAKES 28–34 SMALL BISCUITS

55g/2oz butter
55g/2oz golden syrup
115g/4oz self-raising flour
pinch of salt
½ teaspoon bicarbonate of soda
1 teaspoon ground ginger

1 teaspoon ground cinnamon
½ teaspoon mixed spice
30g/1oz light muscovado sugar

DECORATION (OPTIONAL)
royal icing (see page 270)

1 Preheat the oven to fan 190°C/gas 6. Lightly oil two baking sheets.

2 Put the butter and golden syrup in a saucepan and melt over a low heat. Sift the flour, salt, bicarbonate of soda, spices and sugar into a large bowl. Using a wooden spoon, stir the warm butter into the spiced flour. As soon as it is mixed, gently knead together with your hands and place between two large sheets of greaseproof paper. Gently flatten with a rolling pin and roll out to about 3mm/⅛ in thick. Place on a baking sheet or tray and chill in the fridge for about 10 minutes or until cold and firm.

3 Once cold, stamp out the biscuits using a star-shaped cutter – about 5cm/2in at its widest. Place on the oiled baking sheets, leaving plenty of space between each biscuit. Squish the trimmings together and re-roll between the greaseproof paper. Chill once again and repeat until you've used up the mixture.

4 Bake for 6–8 minutes, until the biscuits are just tinged a darker gold but still soft. Leave to cool and harden slightly on their baking sheets, then, using a palette knife, gently lift on to a wire rack and leave until cold.

5 To decorate, ice the biscuits with royal icing. Use a fine nozzle or homemade piping bag (see page 17) and streak squiggles across each biscuit. Leave the icing to set for 1 hour.

ROYAL ICING

Royal icing can be made in advance and stored in the fridge for several days if you add a small amount of glycerine to stop the icing from becoming very hard. This recipe makes enough to ice the top of a cake or the biscuits on page 268.

1 medium egg white
2 teaspoons lemon juice

250g/9oz icing sugar, sifted
scant ½ teaspoon glycerine (optional)

1 Put the egg white, lemon juice and half of the sifted icing sugar into a bowl. Using a wooden spoon, stir rather than beat the mixture until it is creamy. If you beat the icing, it will create air pockets and make icing more difficult. Slowly add the remaining sugar until the mixture is smooth and forms soft peaks when you pull out the spoon. Add the glycerine, if using.

2 To store the icing, place in a container with a lid, press a sheet of clingfilm over the surface, cover with some damp kitchen paper and seal the container. It will keep in the fridge for up to 4 days. Before use, stir well and, if necessary, add a little more sifted icing sugar.

3 Using a piping bag with a tiny nozzle, push open the piping bag and carefully spoon in the icing. Push the icing down and roll the top over to seal the bag. When piping, keep the bag upright and close to the edge of the biscuit or cake.

4 If you don't have a piping bag with a tiny nozzle, you can make your own by placing one small polythene bag in another and snipping the tiniest corner off to form a nozzle.

STICKY TOFFEE PUDDING

Sticky toffee pudding has become such a British classic it's hard to believe that, like crumble, it was only invented in the twentieth century. No one knows for sure when it was first created. It was popularised by Francis Coulson at Sharrow Bay country house hotel in Ullswater, Cumbria, who first served it in 1960. He is said to have got the idea from a recipe by Mrs Martin of the Old Rectory in Claughton, Lancashire, who in turn based hers on a recipe from a Canadian friend.

SERVES 6

170g/6oz peeled and stoned Medjool dates
120ml/4fl oz very hot freshly made tea, such as
  Earl Grey
85g/3oz butter, softened, plus extra for greasing
140g/5oz light muscovado sugar
½ teaspoon vanilla extract
2 medium eggs
170g/6oz self-raising flour

1 tablespoon good brandy

TOFFEE SAUCE
200g/7oz light muscovado sugar
115g/4oz butter
5 tablespoons double cream
1 tablespoon good brandy (optional)
pinch of salt

1 Preheat the oven to fan 220°C/gas 8. Take six 150ml/5fl oz pudding basins. Using a basin bottom as a template, draw six circles on some baking parchment. Use the top of the basin to draw six more circles, then cut out all the circles. Butter the basins and one side of each paper disc, then line the basin bottoms with the small discs, butter-side up. Put in a deep roasting pan.

2 Finely chop the dates. Place in a small bowl and cover with the piping-hot tea. In a large bowl, beat together the butter and sugar. Add the vanilla, followed by the eggs. Finally, beat in the flour, followed by the brandy, dates and tea.

3 Spoon the mixture into the buttered basins. Top each pudding with a paper disc, butter side down, and cover each with a square of foil tucked tightly around the rim. Pour boiling water into the roasting pan until it comes halfway up the sides of the basins. Cover the pan with

a large sheet of foil and put in the oven. Bake for 30 minutes, or until cooked. To test, insert a skewer into the centre of one of the puddings: if it comes out clean, they're cooked.

4 While the puddings are cooking, make the sauce. Put the sugar in a saucepan with the butter, double cream, brandy and salt, and set over a low heat. Stir occasionally until the sugar has dissolved and the butter has melted. Bring up to the boil and simmer for 4 minutes or until thick and dark.

5 Remove the puddings from the roasting pan and leave to rest for 10 minutes. The sponge will shrink back slightly, making it easy to turn out. Invert each pudding on to a warmed plate. Remove the baking paper and pour some of the hot sauce over each pudding. Serve immediately, with extra sauce.

STICKY GINGER TRAY BAKE

This gorgeous tray bake from the National Trust is a fusion of gingerbread, parkin and flapjack. It's one of those recipes that lines the tummy and keeps the cold out. This cake keeps well in an airtight container, but because it becomes so sticky, you'll need to separate the cut squares with baking parchment to prevent them from squidging together.

MAKES 8 SQUARES

150ml/5fl oz full-fat milk
40g/1½ oz black treacle
80g/2¾ oz butter
55g/2oz plain flour
1½ teaspoons ground ginger

pinch of ground cinnamon
½ teaspoon bicarbonate of soda
115g/4oz light muscovado sugar
40g/1½ oz dark muscovado sugar
100g/3½ oz porridge oats

1 Preheat the oven to fan 150°C/gas 2½. Lightly oil an 18 x 28cm/7 x 11in tray bake tin. Line the base with baking parchment and lightly oil.

2 Put the milk, treacle and butter in a small saucepan. Set over a low heat and stir occasionally until the butter has melted. Leave to cool slightly.

3 Sift the flour, spices and bicarbonate of soda into a large bowl. Mix thoroughly. Mix in the sugars and oats. Give the warm melted ingredients a quick stir and mix into the dry ingredients. Pour into the baking tin and bake for 45 minutes.

4 Leave the ginger tray bake in its tin on a wire rack to cool. Once completely cold, cut into 8 squares. It becomes more gooey with time.

SAFFRON BREAD

Saffron bread dates back to the late fifteenth or early sixteenth century, when a savoury version of it was baked as pre-Lenten bread. Later, sugar, spices, currants and sometimes rose water were added, and it became associated with Easter in the West Country. It can be eaten fresh with clotted cream or toasted with lots of butter.

SERVES 10

large pinch of saffron strands
300ml/10½ fl oz milk
2 teaspoons fast-action dried yeast
500g/1lb 2oz plain flour
pinch of freshly grated nutmeg
1 teaspoon ground cinnamon

½ teaspoon salt
170g/6oz cold butter, diced
85g/3oz caster sugar
170g/6oz currants
85g/3oz chopped mixed peel

1 Using a pestle and mortar or the back of a teaspoon, crush the saffron to a powder and place in a small bowl. Pour the milk into a small pan and set over a medium heat. Scald by bringing to just below boiling point, then remove from the heat and pour on to the saffron. Leave to infuse for 30 minutes. Once it's tepid, sprinkle the yeast over the milk. Gently mix in and leave for 10 minutes or until it looks frothy and smells yeasty.

2 Sift the flour, spices and salt into a food processor. Add the butter and process in short bursts until it forms fine crumbs. Tip into a bowl and mix in the sugar, currants and mixed peel. Make a well in the centre, add the yeasty saffron milk and, using your hand, mix until it forms a soft dough.

3 Turn out on to a clean surface. You may need to add a little flour. Knead until the dough is smooth. Place in a large clean bowl, cover with clingfilm, and leave in a warm, draught-free place for 1–2 hours or until it has doubled in size.

4 Preheat the oven to fan 180°C/gas 5. Lightly grease a 23cm/9in round cake tin with a removable base.

5 Turn the dough out and lightly knead before shaping into a slightly flattened round. Place in the cake tin, place in a plastic bag, and leave to rise for 1 hour.

6 Bake for 1 hour or until well risen and golden. Remove and leave to cool slightly on a wire rack before turning out.

BRANDY SEED CAKE

Seed cakes were popular in the seventeenth, eighteenth and nineteenth centuries. The early recipes used yeast as the raising agent, but gradually egg-risen sponges replaced them. The posthumous 1758 edition of Eliza Smith's *The Compleat Housewife* gives recipes for both. She uses sack (a type of dry wine), caraway comfits (which are sugared) and lots of candied bitter orange peel. Some recipes include ground almonds or other spices such as ginger, mace and allspice.

SERVES 8

225g/8oz butter, softened
225g/8oz caster sugar
5 medium eggs, separated
225g/8oz plain flour, sifted
¼ teaspoon freshly grated nutmeg

pinch of ground mace
2 teaspoons caraway seeds
85g/3oz chopped mixed peel
2 tablespoons brandy
sugar lumps, roughly crushed with a rolling pin

1 Preheat the oven to fan 170°C/gas 4. Grease a 18cm/7in square cake tin with a removable base. Line the base with baking parchment and lightly oil.

2 In a large bowl, beat the butter and caster sugar together until pale and fluffy. Gradually beat in the egg yolks, a little at a time, adding a little flour if the mixture looks as though it might separate. Mix in the spices, caraway seeds, mixed peel and brandy.

3 In a separate bowl, whisk the egg whites until they form soft peaks. Using a flat metal spoon, fold some of the flour into the butter, followed by some of the whisked egg white. Repeat until both are folded into the cake mixture.

4 Transfer the mixture into the prepared cake tin. Strew with the roughly crushed sugar lumps and bake for 1 hour or until springy to touch. To test, insert a skewer into the centre of the cake: it should come out clean. Leave to cool in the tin for 5 minutes, then turn out on to a wire rack and leave until cold.

DRIED FRUIT

Every time you go to your cupboard to weigh out some sultanas or currants, you are following in the footsteps of countless English cooks before you, stretching back to at least the Norman Conquest. For centuries, these sweet fruits have been added to foods on high days and holidays.

Raisins, sultanas and currants are all dried grapes. Sultanas usually refer to the largest form of dried grape and can vary in colour from green to dark brown. Currants are tiny dried black grapes that were originally imported from Corinth in Greece, but now refer to many different varieties of small dark grapes. All other dried grapes tend to be called raisins; they vary in size and colour. Each adds a slightly different texture, flavour and colour to a dish.

In the past, other dried fruits such as prunes, dates and figs were added to raisins in cakes, pastries and puddings, along with candied peel. Keen cooks might enjoy making their own candied peel – it really does taste wonderful. You can use thick-pithed oranges and lemons or Seville oranges – and if you're lucky enough to find them, fresh citrons. Citrons have a superb lemon flavour, thick pith and little flesh and are traditionally used in mixed peel. However if, like me, you tend to use ready-chopped mixed peel, you can enhance its flavour by adding a little finely grated lemon or orange zest.

Glacé cherries (stoned maraschino cherries candied in sugar syrup) should be rinsed from their sticky sugar syrup then patted dry and halved. This will help prevent them from sinking to the bottom of the cake.

There is no doubt that domestic bakers are benefiting from the current fashion for eating dried fruits as a healthy snack. We can choose from all manner of dried and semi-dried fruits, from apples and pears to cranberries, cherries and blueberries. Organic dried fruit is particularly good in recipes in which you need to macerate the dried fruit. It tends to be slightly drier than its non-organic counterparts and therefore absorbs more flavoursome liquid when soaking. All dried fruit should be stored in an airtight container in a cool, dark place.

WHISKY LUNCHEON CAKE

There was a time, not so long ago, when fruit cake such as this was regularly served at the end of lunch or as part of a picnic. It seems the perfect time to revive this pre-war tradition, as slices of fruit cake make an excellent addition to a packed lunch for work. If you're always in a rush in the morning, the day after baking, slice the cake, and wrap and freeze individual slices for your lunch box. The frozen cake will keep the rest of your lunch cool as it defrosts.

MAKES 8 SLICES

225g/8oz mixed sultanas, raisins and currants
70g/2½ oz glacé cherries, halved
30g/1oz chopped mixed peel
100ml/3½ fl oz whisky, plus 3 tablespoons
115g/4oz butter, softened
115g/4oz light muscovado sugar
1 teaspoon mixed spice

finely grated zest of 1 orange
finely grated zest of 1 lemon, plus 3 tablespoons
    lemon juice
1 medium egg, beaten
150g/5½ oz plain flour
⅓ teaspoon bicarbonate of soda
3 tablespoons milk

1 Mix together all the dried fruit and 100ml/3½ fl oz whisky in a bowl. Cover and leave to soak for 24 hours.

2 Preheat the oven to fan 130°C/gas 1. Lightly oil a 900g/2lb non-stick loaf tin. Line the base and ends with a strip of baking parchment.

3 In a large bowl, beat together the butter, sugar, mixed spice, orange and lemon zest until pale and fluffy, then gradually beat in the egg. Sift the flour and bicarbonate of soda together into a small bowl, mix thoroughly, then beat into the butter mixture. Stir in the whisky-soaked fruit, including all the whisky, followed by the lemon juice and milk.

4 Spoon into the loaf tin and bake for 2 hours or until a knife inserted into the centre comes out clean. Transfer the tin to a wire rack and leave for 5 minutes, then turn out the cake. Lightly pierce the cake with a skewer and carefully drizzle the 3 tablespoons of whisky into the warm cake. Leave until cold, then wrap in foil and store. This cake will keep well for up to a week.

CHRISTMAS CAKE

This is my favourite Christmas cake recipe. These days, most rich fruit cakes are quite heavy, but in the past British cooks had used all sorts of techniques to lighten their cakes. Intrigued by this idea, I devised this recipe, in which the eggs are separated and the whisked whites folded into the cake batter. The cake itself is modelled on the ultra-delicious dark Caribbean style of fruit cake, hence the rum, Angostura bitters and dark muscovado sugar.

SERVES ABOUT 12

170g/6oz currants
170g/6oz sultanas
170g/6oz raisins
125g/4½ oz prunes, roughly chopped
60g/2¼ oz mixed peel, roughly chopped
100g/3½ oz glacé cherries
300ml/10½ fl oz dark rum, plus extra for feeding
    the cake
about 100ml/3½ fl oz apple brandy or Calvados
250g/9oz plain flour, sifted
¾ teaspoon bicarbonate of soda
170g/6oz butter
170g/6oz dark muscovado sugar

½ teaspoon each ground cinnamon, mixed spice
    and ground nutmeg
1 teaspoon Angostura bitters
5 medium eggs, separated
100g/3½ oz black treacle
finely grated zest and juice of 1 lemon
finely grated zest of 1 small orange

COVERING AND ICING
700g/1lb 9oz white marzipan
icing sugar for dusting
4 tablespoons red currant jelly, warmed
900g/2lb ready-to-roll fondant icing

1 Mix together the currants, sultanas, raisins, prunes, mixed peel and cherries in a large bowl. Tip into a plastic container with a lid and mix in 300ml/10½ fl oz rum. Seal and leave for a minimum of 2 days. You can soak the fruit for a week. Mix regularly to ensure that all the fruit can absorb the alcohol.

2 Preheat the oven to fan 130°C/gas 1. Lightly oil a large round 23cm/9in cake tin. Turn to page 19 and follow the instructions on how to line a round cake tin.

3 Strain the macerated dried fruit and save any remaining sticky rum juice. Measure it and add enough apple brandy to make up to 150ml/5fl oz. Set aside.

4 Sift the flour and bicarbonate of soda into a small bowl. Mix thoroughly. In a large bowl, beat the butter and sugar until fluffy. Gradually beat in the spices, Angostura bitters and egg yolks, followed by the treacle, grated citrus zest and lemon juice. Mix in half the flour, half the macerated fruit and half the rum and apple brandy mixture, then add the remaining fruit, followed by the flour and rum and apple brandy.

5 Quickly whisk the egg whites until they form stiff peaks. Fold into the cake mixture and immediately transfer to the lined cake tin, making a slight dip in the middle of the cake mixture. Bake for 40 minutes, then lightly cover the top of the cake with a greaseproof paper disc. As all ovens vary slightly in temperature, check to see if the cake is done after 2½ hours: insert a skewer into the centre of the cake, and if it comes out clean, the cake is ready. It may need up to 3½ hours. Remove from the oven and leave to cool in its tin.

6 When it is completely cold, remove from the tin. Peel away the baking paper and place on a large sheet of foil. Pierce the top of the cake with a fine skewer. Using a spoon, drizzle in about 3 tablespoons rum. Tightly wrap in the foil and store in an airtight tin (or keep tightly wrapped in foil). Continue to feed the cake with rum every day or so, until you are satisfied that it is sufficiently rich and alcoholic.

7 To apply the marzipan, turn the cake upside down on a clean surface so that its flat bottom becomes the top. Cut the marzipan in half. Divide one piece in half again and shape into two sausages, each approximately half the circumference of the cake. Sprinkle a clean work surface with icing sugar and then roll out the marzipan 'sausages' until they are as wide as the cake is high.

8 Brush the sides of the cake thoroughly with the warmed red currant jelly. Carefully apply the rolled marzipan to the sides of the cake, patting and trimming as necessary. Knead the remaining marzipan into a ball, roll out and cut out a disc large enough to cover the top of the cake. Brush the top of the cake with red currant jelly and gently fit the marzipan on top of the cake. Leave to dry out for a minimum of 3 hours before icing the cake. You can leave it overnight.

9 To ice the cake, lightly knead the icing until soft and malleable. Shape it into a large ball and place on a work surface dusted with icing sugar. Shape the ball into a disc and roll it out, rotating the icing like the hands of a clock – 5 minutes between every roll of the pin – until you have a large disc about 5mm/¼ in thick and 42cm/17in diameter. This should be enough to cover the top and sides of the cake. Brush the marzipanned surface of the cake with just-boiled water so that it is sticky, then partially roll the icing around the rolling pin, lift it over the cake and unroll. Gently smooth the icing over the top and sides of the cake, smoothing out any pleats as you do so. Trim the bottom of the cake and decorate as you please. This cake keeps well for up to 2 months.

MINCE PIES

This recipe comes from Sara Paston-Williams' wonderful *The National Trust Book of Christmas and Festive Day Recipes* (1981); she uses an almond pastry. Her recipe for mincemeat is on page 284.

If you're a mince pie fan, it's worth remembering that it is considered lucky to eat twelve pies between Christmas and Twelfth Day – presumably one a day. No wonder Oliver Cromwell passed an Act of Parliament in 1650 authorising the imprisonment of anyone found guilty of eating a currant pie. Apparently, Christmas mince pies were considered too indulgent and hinted at paganism.

MAKES ABOUT 20

ALMOND PASTRY
340g/12oz plain flour, sifted
225g/8oz cold butter, diced
85g/3oz ground almonds
85g/3oz caster sugar
2 medium egg yolks
2 tablespoons cold water

FILLING AND TOPPING
450g/1lb home-made mincemeat (see page 284)
2 tablespoons brandy or rum
1 egg white, beaten
caster sugar and icing sugar for sprinkling

1 To make the almond pastry, put the flour and butter into a food processor. Process in short bursts until the mixture forms fine crumbs. Tip into a bowl and stir in the ground almonds and sugar. Add the egg yolks and enough cold water to make a firm paste. Cover and chill for 1 hour.

2 Meanwhile, mix the mincemeat with the brandy or rum. Preheat the oven to fan 190°C/gas 6. Lightly grease twenty 6cm/2½ in patty tins (see bun tray, page 15).

3 Roll out the pastry to about 3mm/⅛ in thick. Stamp out half of it into 7.5cm/3in diameter discs and half into 6cm/2½ in width stars. Line the greased tins with the pastry discs. Lightly brush the rims with a little beaten egg white, then fill with mincemeat to the level of the pastry edges. Don't be tempted to overfill or the mincemeat will boil out.

4 Cover each tart with a pastry star, lightly pressing it on to the egg white-brushed rim. Brush the stars with beaten egg white and sprinkle with caster sugar. Bake for 25–30 minutes, until golden brown.

5 Cool on a wire rack. When cold, sprinkle with more caster sugar or sifted icing sugar.

6 To serve, reheat in a warm oven. Make sure you don't overheat, because mincemeat retains heat and can easily burn your mouth.

MINCEMEAT

According to Sara Paston-Williams in *The National Trust Book of Christmas and Festive Day Recipes* (1981), by Elizabethan times 'shred' or 'minced' pies had become part of traditional English Christmas fare. Originally, mutton or beef meat and suet would be shredded and mixed together with cloves, mace, pepper and saffron, along with dried fruits. Over time, apples and brandy or sack (a form of dry white wine) were added, and the meat was omitted. Here is her recipe.

MAKES ABOUT 3.6KG/8LB

2 tablespoons whole almonds in their skins
450g/1lb cooking apples
450g/1lb beef or vegetarian suet
225g/8oz chopped mixed peel
450g/1lb raisins
450g/1lb sultanas

450g/1lb currants
340g/12oz light muscovado sugar
1 teaspoon mixed spice
finely grated zest and juice of 1 lemon
150ml/5fl oz rum, brandy or whisky

1 Blanch the almonds: cover with boiling water, leave for 5 minutes, then drain and slip out of their skins. Rinse to preserve their colour, pat dry and slice lengthways, using a small sharp knife. Place the shredded almonds in a large bowl.

2 Peel, core and roughly grate the apples. Mix into the almonds, together with the suet, mixed peel, raisins, sultanas, currants, muscovado sugar, mixed spice, lemon zest and juice and rum, brandy or whisky.

3 Sterilise your jam jars by washing them in hot soapy water, rinsing in very hot water and then placing them in a cool oven (fan 130°C/gas 1) to dry. Alternatively, wash in the dishwasher then leave to dry with the dishwasher door partially open.

4 Pack the mincemeat into the sterilised jars. Cover with clean lids or cellophane jam pot covers. Label and store for at least one month before using to allow the flavours to mature. Use within three months. Once you've opened a jar, store in the fridge.

MADEIRA CAKE

This fragrant, buttery cake takes its name from the eighteenth-century custom of enjoying a slice of plain cake with a mid-morning glass of Madeira – a practice well worth reviving if your guests are a little trying. However, the term only became commonplace in the late nineteenth century and usually referred to a butter sponge flavoured with lemon. This recipe improves if eaten the next day. It also freezes well.

SERVES 8

170g/6oz butter, softened
170g/6oz caster sugar, plus extra to serve
finely grated zest of 1 orange
finely grated zest of 1 lemon, plus 1 tablespoon
    lemon juice

4 medium eggs, beaten
170g/6oz self-raising flour, sifted
pinch of salt
55g/2oz chopped mixed peel

1 Preheat the oven to fan 170°C/gas 4. Lightly grease an 18cm/7in cake tin with a removable base. Line the base with baking parchment and lightly grease the parchment.

2 Beat the butter, sugar, orange and lemon zest together until pale and fluffy. You can do this in a food processor if you like. Still beating, gradually add the eggs, a little at a time, waiting until the egg is fully incorporated before adding some more. Transfer to a mixing bowl. Beat in the lemon juice, then mix in the flour, salt and mixed peel.

3 Spoon the mixture into the cake tin and bake for about 1 hour or until golden and springy to the touch. If the cake is browning too quickly, loosely cover the top with foil, but remember to remove it shortly before the end of cooking. Test by inserting a skewer into the centre of the cake: if it comes out clean, the cake is cooked.

4 Put the cake tin on a wire rack and leave for 15 minutes. Then remove the cake from its tin and turn upside down to flatten the cake slightly. After 10 minutes, turn over and sprinkle with sugar. Once cold, wrap in foil.

SPICED YULE BREAD

Before the invention of the cake ring in the seventeenth century, celebratory spicy fruit cakes were made by enriching a yeast-risen dough with butter, lard and eggs. This addictively spicy recipe from the National Trust is a perfect example.

MAKES A 900G/2LB LOAF

250ml/9fl oz tepid milk
3 teaspoons fast-action dried yeast
450g/1lb plain flour
½ teaspoon salt
2 teaspoons mixed spice
55g/2oz cold butter, diced

55g/2oz cold lard, diced
115g/4oz caster sugar
115g/4oz currants
115g/4oz raisins
55g/2oz chopped mixed peel
1 medium egg, beaten

1 Put 100ml/3½ fl oz of the tepid milk in a bowl and sprinkle the yeast over the milk. Gently mix and leave for 10 minutes or until it has dissolved, smells of fresh yeast and looks frothy.

2 Sift the flour, salt and spice into a food processor. Add the diced butter and lard and whiz in short bursts until the mixture resembles fine breadcrumbs. Tip into a large mixing bowl and mix in the caster sugar, dried fruit and peel, followed by the beaten egg.

3 Mix the yeasty milk into the flour mixture. Rinse the yeast bowl with the remaining tepid milk. Add it gradually to the dough, until it is soft but not too sticky. Turn out on to a lightly floured surface and knead for

5 minutes. Place in a large clean bowl, cover with clingfilm and leave in a warm, draught-free place for about 2 hours or until it has almost doubled in size.

4 Preheat the oven to fan 190°C/gas 6. Lightly oil a 900g/2lb loaf tin. Turn the dough on to a clean surface. Shape it into a loaf and place in the oiled loaf tin. Place in an inflated plastic bag and leave in a warm place for 30 minutes or until puffy and slightly risen in the tin.

5 Bake for 60 minutes or until risen and golden brown. To test, turn out of its tin and tap the bottom: if it sounds hollow, it's cooked. Leave to cool on a wire rack. This bread freezes well.

ECCLES CAKES

There is much discussion as to the origin of Eccles cakes and the best way to make them. Suffice it to say that they date back to the eighteenth century and that a cake of that name was traditionally made for wakes week, a religious festival commemorating the founding of the local church. Most importantly, everyone still loves them, and you can find them on the menu of many National Trust properties, such as Bateman's, Rudyard Kipling's home in Burwash in the Sussex Weald.

MAKES 10–12 CAKES

225g/8oz rough puff pastry (see page 83)
30g/1oz butter
30g/1oz light muscovado sugar
1 teaspoon mixed spice
½ teaspoon ground nutmeg

115g/4oz currants
30g/1oz chopped mixed peel
1 egg white, roughly beaten
2 tablespoons caster sugar

1 Grease two baking sheets. In a small saucepan, melt the butter with the muscovado sugar and spices. Mix in the currants and mixed peel and leave until cold.

2 On a lightly floured surface, roll out the pastry to about 5mm/¼ in thick. Cut out circles using a 10cm/4in diameter cutter, or use a saucer or cup if you don't have a big enough cutter. I use the metal round tin that holds my set of scone cutters.

3 Place a generous teaspoonful of the spicy currant mixture in the centre of each pastry disc. Dampen the edges of the first pastry disc with a little water. Gather the edges together and pinch to seal well. Turn over so that the join is underneath and lightly roll out the cake on a floured surface, so that the currants just show through the pastry. Keep your rolling pin well floured as you do so. Place on a baking sheet and repeat the process with the remaining Eccles cakes. Chill for 10–15 minutes.

4 Preheat the oven to fan 220°C/gas 8. Make two or three slits on top of each cake, brush with the beaten egg white and dredge with caster sugar. Bake for 10–15 minutes until crisp and golden. Cool on a wire rack.

COFFEE & TEA

No kitchen is complete without some good tea and coffee. Today, we take them for granted, but they were once so valuable they were kept locked away. Both were introduced into England in the second half of the seventeenth century.

Tea has never really taken off as a flavouring in Britain, despite its popularity as a drink. There are a few recipes for tea-infused baked creams from the eighteenth century, when tea was still very expensive and baked creams were *à la mode*. By the nineteenth century, tea is barely mentioned in cookbooks. One exception is Mrs Marshall's superb *The Book of Ices* (1885), in which she gives recipes for tea (and coffee) ices. In the twentieth century, tea's main use in baking was to soak dried fruit for cakes and bread – adding colour and a slight bitterness to recipes such as spiced fruit brack (see page 293).

Tea is currently enjoying a culinary renaissance, in part influenced by the British Indian taste for sweetened and spiced milky tea. This flavour combination works well in bread and butter pudding or in a twenty-first-century interpretation of a baked custard, spiced tea creams (see page 292).

Coffee did not become a popular culinary flavouring until the twentieth century, when it was added to cakes and whipped cream puddings. Today it is used in all manner of creamy baked foods, such as coffee crème caramel, coffee crème brûlée and coffee bread and butter pudding (see page 291). In cakes, it is particularly irresistible in the form of butter cream, whether in plain sponges (see page 37), walnut cakes or as a topping for chocolate cupcakes.

COFFEE BREAD AND BUTTER PUDDING

English recipes for bread and butter pudding first appeared in the 1720s, when it was made with fresh buttered bread, sprinkled with currants and baked with a nutmeg-flavoured custard. Since then, there have been countless variations. For example, the bread can be replaced by brioche, and the custard can be infused with different ingredients such as chocolate or saffron.

SERVES 6

425ml/15fl oz milk
425ml/15fl oz double cream
4 tablespoons medium-ground coffee beans
115g/4oz granulated sugar, plus 1 tablespoon
    for sprinkling

55g/2oz butter, softened, plus extra for greasing
9 thick slices good-quality white bread
85g/3oz raisins
2 medium eggs
3 medium egg yolks

1 Put the milk, cream, coffee and 115/4oz granulated sugar in a saucepan. Set over a medium heat and bring to the boil, then remove from the heat, stir once and leave to infuse for 30 minutes.

2 Meanwhile, liberally butter a 20 x 30cm/8 x 12in oval shallow ovenproof dish, or a rectangular dish of a similar size. Liberally butter the bread, cut off the crusts and cut into halves or quarters. Arrange half of the bread in the buttered dish, buttered side up, and sprinkle with the raisins. Cover with the remaining bread, buttered side up.

3 Lightly beat the whole eggs and yolks together, then strain through a sieve into a large jug. Strain the coffee cream through a fine sieve into the eggs. Mix thoroughly and pour over the buttered bread. Cover and chill for 30 minutes, so that the custard has time to soak into the bread.

4 Preheat the oven to fan 170°C/gas 4. Sprinkle the top of the bread with 1 tablespoon of sugar. Place in a roasting pan and add enough just-boiled water to come halfway up the side of the dish. Bake for 45 minutes or until the custard is set and the top is flecked golden. Serve hot, warm or at room temperature.

SPICED TEA CREAMS

Tea tastes wonderful combined with cardamom, cinnamon, cloves and cream. However, as baked cream puddings tend to be very rich, I've hidden some Armagnac-soaked prunes at the bottom of these. The prunes need to be macerated for at least 24 hours but taste amazing if stored for several weeks, so I've doubled the prune quantities so that you can make this recipe twice if you wish. Be warned, though, it's hard not to raid the jar.

SERVES 4

285ml/10fl oz single cream
4 green cardamom pods, bruised
4 cloves
1 cinnamon stick, broken in half
85g/3oz unrefined caster sugar
1 tablespoon Assam tea leaves
1 medium egg, strained
3 medium egg yolks, strained

FOR THE BRANDY PRUNES
115g/4oz ready-to-eat stoned prunes
70ml/2½ fl oz Armagnac
1½ tablespoons unrefined caster sugar
½ cinnamon stick, broken in half

1 To make the brandy prunes, first sterilise a small jar (see step 3, elderberry jelly on page 243) or other sealable container. Halve the prunes and place in a small non-corrosive saucepan with the Armagnac, sugar and cinnamon. Set over a low heat, stirring occasionally, until the sugar has dissolved, then slowly bring to the boil. As soon as it bubbles briskly, tip the mixture into the sterilised container. Leave for a minimum of 24 hours. The prunes can be stored at room temperature, but shake regularly.

2 Preheat the oven to fan 180°C/gas 5. Lightly oil four 150ml/5fl oz ramekin dishes and place on kitchen paper in a deep roasting pan.

3 Put the cream, cardamom pods, cloves, cinnamon and sugar in a small saucepan. Set over a low heat and let it slowly come up to the boil. Add the tea, remove from the heat, and leave to infuse for 10 minutes. Scald once

again so that the cream just bubbles at the rim of the pan. Then leave to infuse until tepid. Strain into a jug. Lightly beat the whole egg and yolks together. Strain the eggs through a sieve into the tepid cream. Mix thoroughly.

4 Remove about half the prunes from their brandy syrup and roughly dice. Divide between the ramekins, so that you have a single layer of diced prunes in the bottom of each dish.

5 Divide the cream mixture evenly between the ramekins. Pour enough boiling water into the roasting pan to come halfway up the sides of the ramekins. Cover the pan with foil. Place in the oven and bake for 35 minutes or until the custards are just set with a slight wobble. Serve warm or at room temperature.

SPICED FRUIT BRACK

This fruit cake is made without any fat. Instead, the dried fruit is soaked in tea and the cake is aerated by a raising agent and an egg. The tea adds a wonderful depth of flavour and makes the fruit extra moist. This recipe keeps well wrapped in foil and freezes well. If you want to use it in a lunch box, wrap individual slices in clingfilm and freeze.

MAKES 10 SLICES

115g/4oz sultanas
150g/5½ oz currants
55g/2oz chopped mixed peel
85g/3oz light muscovado sugar
finely grated zest of 2 lemons
115g/4oz Chinese stem ginger (about 5 knobs),
    drained of its syrup

300ml/10½ fl oz strong hot tea, such as Darjeeling
1 medium egg, beaten
2 teaspoons ground ginger
½ teaspoon mixed spice
1¼ teaspoons baking powder
285g/10oz plain flour

1 Place the sultanas, currants, mixed peel, sugar and lemon zest in a non-reactive bowl. Cut the stem ginger into dice about the same size as the currants. Mix into the dried fruit. Stir the hot tea into the fruit, cover the bowl and leave overnight or up to 24 hours. The longer the fruit soaks the more succulent the cake, but if you're in a rush a few hours will still produce a decent cake.

2 The next day, preheat the oven to fan 160°C/gas 3. Lightly grease a 900g/2lb loaf tin and line the base and ends with a strip of baking parchment.

3 Using a wooden spoon, stir the beaten egg into the tea-soaked fruit. Sift together the ground ginger, mixed spice, baking powder and plain flour. Mix together, then stir into the fruit and spoon into the loaf tin. Bake for 1½ hours or until cooked through. Test by inserting a skewer: if it comes out clean, the cake is cooked. Leave in its tin on a wire rack until tepid, then turn out and wrap once cold.

CHOCOLATE

Had you stepped into a larder some forty-odd years ago, you would have seen, neatly stacked beside the tea, coffee and sugar, a well-used carton of cocoa and a bar of dark chocolate. Depending on the cook's taste, the latter would have been either Bournville or Chocolat Menier. Both cocoa and chocolate were used to flavour all manner of cakes, biscuits and puddings.

Today, supermarkets offer dozens of different types of chocolate. Every label is packed with information, from cocoa percentage and origin, to type of cocoa bean and method of production. It's wonderful to have so much choice, but it can be confusing when you are looking for a chocolate to bake with.

The first thing to remember is that a high cocoa percentage is not automatically an indication of good quality, merely a statement of fact, like the percentage of alcohol on a bottle of wine. The quality of the beans and method of production are far more important. However, a named cocoa bean or the words 'single estate' or 'organic' do not necessarily make one chocolate superior to another.

It is worth doing a little research to find the right chocolate, as your choice will affect the quality of your baked dishes, especially when the main ingredient is chocolate. Look for a bar that is a rich mahogany colour rather than black: the latter is likely to be made from Forastero beans, which have a strong earthy flavour, or to have been over-roasted, which can leave an unpleasant bitter taste. The chocolate bar should snap – not splinter or crumble – when broken and smell good. Once in your mouth, it should melt into a silky texture and release a lovely aroma.

As a general rule, dark chocolate for eating should contain at least 60 per cent cocoa solids and milk chocolate at least 30 per cent. However, when it comes to baking, you don't want a dark chocolate with too high a proportion of cocoa solids as these can make a cake or pudding taste bitter. Instead you want a chocolate with a good balance of cocoa solids and cocoa butter. This allows the chocolate to melt to a creamy consistency, which in turn helps a cake rise properly and produces a luscious (as opposed to granular) chocolate icing. Cheaper brands often replace cocoa butter with vegetable oil, so you will need to check the label. In her classic *Baking Bible* (2009), Mary Berry recommends using a plain chocolate with 39 per cent cocoa solids for cakes.

Good-quality milk chocolate should contain whole (full-cream) milk. Generally it is best used as a last-minute addition, such as in the banana choc chip muffins on page 301. White chocolate is even sweeter and should be made solely from cocoa butter. Avoid cheap brands that use vegetable oil. Some brands are heavily flavoured with vanilla, so factor that in when spicing a dish.

Lastly, no kitchen cupboard should be without a good-quality cocoa powder – not to be confused with drinking chocolate. Cocoa powder is made from unsweetened cocoa solids; it can add extra depth of flavour when combined with chocolate in a dish.

CHOCOLATE FUDGE CAKE

Who can resist an over-the-top gooey chocolate cake? This is one of my favourite recipes.

SERVES 10

150g/5½ oz dark chocolate, chopped
400g/14oz dark muscovado sugar
225ml/8fl oz full-fat milk
250g/9oz plain flour
1½ teaspoons baking powder
3 tablespoons cocoa powder
pinch of salt

150g/5½ oz butter, softened
3 medium eggs, beaten
¼ teaspoon vanilla extract

CHOCOLATE GANACHE
340g/12oz dark chocolate, chopped
300ml/10½ fl oz single cream

1 Preheat the oven to fan 160°C/gas 3. Lightly oil two 20cm/8in sandwich tins. Line the base of each with baking parchment and lightly oil.

2 Put the chocolate, half the sugar and about two-thirds of the milk in a saucepan. Set over a low heat and gently stir until the chocolate has melted and the sugar has dissolved. Remove from the heat and set aside.

3 Sift together the flour, baking powder, cocoa powder and salt. Mix thoroughly and set aside. Put the butter and remaining sugar in a large mixing bowl and beat until pale and creamy, using a wooden spoon or electric whisk.

4 Gradually beat in the eggs, a little at a time, until light and fluffy – adding a couple of tablespoons of the flour mixture if it looks as though the mixture is about to separate. Beat in the vanilla extract. Then, using a flat metal spoon, gently fold in the flour mixture, in three batches, alternating with the remaining cold milk. Finally, fold in the warm chocolate mixture.

5 Divide between the prepared tins and bake for 40 minutes or until the sponge springs back when lightly pressed. Test by inserting a skewer into the centre of the cake: if it comes out clean, the cake is cooked. Cool the cakes in their tins on a wire rack for 10 minutes, then turn out and peel off the baking paper.

6 Meanwhile, make the chocolate ganache. Put the chocolate in a bowl that will neatly fit over a pan of just-boiled water (off the heat). You may need to replace the boiling water to allow the chocolate to melt. Once the chocolate has melted, put the cream in a small saucepan, bring to the boil, and pour into the melted chocolate. Using a wooden spoon, beat thoroughly until the mixture is smooth and glossy. Leave to cool.

7 Once both the cake and the ganache are at room temperature, sandwich the two chocolate sponges together with ganache, then cover with the remaining ganache. Leave in a cool place to set. This will take several hours.

FRENCH CHOCOLATE CAKE (GF)

This is a cake that tastes even better the day after it's made. It's an elegant cake that you might serve for tea after dainty sandwiches and miniature savoury scones. I normally make this with plain white flour, but you could make it with gluten-free flour instead.

SERVES 6

115g/4oz dark chocolate, chopped
55g/2oz butter, diced
3 medium eggs, separated
85g/3oz caster sugar

pinch of salt
few drops of vanilla extract
20g/¾ oz plain or gluten-free flour
icing sugar for dusting

1 Preheat the oven to fan 180°C/gas 5. Lightly oil a 20cm/8in spring-form cake tin. Line the base with baking parchment and lightly oil.

2 Put the chocolate in a bowl that will neatly fit over a pan of just-boiled water (off the heat). You may need to replace the boiling water to allow the chocolate to melt. Once the chocolate has melted, add the butter and stir until it has melted. Remove the bowl from the hot water and leave to cool slightly.

3 In a large bowl, whisk the egg yolks with the caster sugar and mix in a pinch of salt, then fold in the tepid chocolate and butter mixture and the vanilla, using a metal spoon. Quickly sift the flour over the chocolate mixture and fold it in. Immediately, in a clean dry bowl, whisk the egg whites until they form soft peaks, and then fold them into the chocolate mixture.

4 Pour the mixture into the prepared tin and bake for about 25 minutes. The cake will puff up and form a slight crust as it cooks. Test by inserting a skewer into the centre of the cake: if it comes out almost clean, the cake is ready.

5 Leave to cool in its tin on a wire rack. When cold, carefully unclip the tin and turn out. The cake is very delicate, so take care when peeling off the baking paper. Dust with icing sugar before serving.

BANANA CHOC CHIP MUFFINS

The key to fluffy muffins is speed and lightness of hand. Measure out all the ingredients before you start (a golden rule in baking) and try to limit your 'folding in' to about 8–10 strokes. You can adapt this basic muffin recipe to other flavourings both sweet and savoury, for example, apple and blueberry muffins (page 194) and cheese and marigold muffins (page 134). You can replace the milk chocolate here with dark chocolate chips or even white chocolate.

MAKES 12 MUFFINS

115g/4oz butter
115g/4oz light muscovado sugar
150ml/5fl oz cold milk
2 medium eggs, beaten
½ teaspoon vanilla extract

250g/9oz self-raising flour
½ teaspoon bicarbonate of soda
pinch of salt
55g/2oz milk chocolate chips
1 medium banana, diced

1 Preheat the oven to fan 170°C/gas 4. Place 12 paper muffin cases in a muffin tray.

2 Melt the butter in a saucepan with the sugar. Cool slightly. Add the milk, followed by the eggs and vanilla.

3 Sift the flour, bicarbonate of soda and salt into a large mixing bowl. Add the chocolate chips and diced banana. Using a metal spoon, quickly fold in the milk mixture, using as few strokes as possible. Do not over-mix.

4 Quickly spoon the mixture into the muffin cases and bake for 20–25 minutes or until cooked. Test by inserting a skewer: if it comes out clean, aside from the melted chocolate, they're ready. Cool on a wire rack.

CHOCOLATE CHIP COOKIES

Every child will love these classic gooey vanilla-flavoured cookies. I've used white chocolate here, but you could replace it with dark or milk chocolate. They will keep for a week in an airtight tin – if you can resist them that long.

MAKES ABOUT 25 COOKIES

100g/3½ oz white chocolate
115g/4oz butter, softened
85g/3oz caster sugar
55g/2oz light muscovado sugar

½ teaspoon vanilla extract
1 large egg, beaten
140g/5oz self-raising flour, sifted

1 Preheat the oven to fan 190°C/gas 6. Lightly grease three baking sheets and arrange your oven shelves so that you can easily slip in the three baking sheets at the same time.

2 Cut the white chocolate into 5mm/¼ in chunks. In a food processor, beat the butter, caster sugar and muscovado sugar together until pale and fluffy. Beat in the vanilla and gradually beat in the egg. Scrape the mixture into a mixing bowl. Using a wooden spoon, stir in the flour, followed by the chocolate.

3 Spoon dessertspoonfuls of the mixture on to the baking sheets, leaving plenty of space between each cookie – they spread out as they cook.

4 Bake for 8–10 minutes or until pale gold. You don't want them to over-cook and darken, otherwise they will be too hard when you eat them. Leave to cool slightly on their baking sheets for 5–10 minutes. Then use a palette knife to transfer them to a wire rack. Eat warm or cold. They should be slightly chewy.

CHOCOLATE VIOLET ÉCLAIRS

These delicious éclairs are best eaten on the day they're made. You can chill and eat them the next day – they'll be a bit softer. You can buy crystallised violets from specialist delicatessens and online baking shops. If you wish, you can replace the kirsch with crème de violette, which can be found in some specialist drink shops. Alternatively, you can flavour the cream with the finely grated zest of an orange – or simply use plain whipped cream.

MAKES 12 ÉCLAIRS

½ quantity choux pastry (see page 85)

VIOLET CREAM FILLING
55g/2oz crystallised violets
285ml/10fl oz double cream
3 tablespoons kirsch

CHOCOLATE ICING
55g/2oz dark chocolate, roughly chopped
15g/½ oz butter, diced
2 tablespoons water
3 tablespoons icing sugar, sifted

1 To make the éclairs, follow the recipe on page 85, but use half the quantities. Reserve 12 crystallised violets for decoration and roughly crush the remaining violets.

2 Once the éclairs are completely cold, make the violet cream filling. Pour the cream and kirsch into a large bowl. Whisk until the cream forms soft peaks. Fold the crushed crystallised violets into the cream. Transfer to a piping bag with a 1cm/½ in plain nozzle. Fill each éclair with some cream.

3 To make the chocolate icing, put the chocolate, butter and water in a large bowl that fits snugly over a pan of just-boiled water (off the heat). Stir occasionally until the chocolate and butter have melted. You may need to replace the boiling water to allow them to melt. Remove the bowl from the pan and beat in the sifted icing sugar. Once the icing is smooth, spoon it over the top of each éclair. Decorate with a single crystallised violet. Leave to set.

HONEY

Wander around the gardens at Packwood House in Warwickshire, and you will notice small niches in the wall. These are bee-boles, built in 1756 to shelter the woven straw skeps that housed the bees. Wooden beehives were not introduced until the nineteenth century. Look carefully, and you will find bee-boles everywhere, in old orchard walls, beside rural cottage gardens and tucked into the walls of outbuildings. For centuries, honey has been an essential ingredient in every home, even after sugar replaced it as the main sweetener in the sixteenth century.

It's easy to understand why. The floral notes of a spoonful of lime (linden) flower or apple blossom honey transport you into the soft dappled world of early summer. No cook would willingly renounce such a wonderful ingredient;

they simply changed its usage. Honey became an accompaniment or flavouring to food, rather than the primary sweetener.

These days, honey can be divided into two main categories: mass-produced and artisan. The former is made by blending different honeys and subjecting them to flash heating to ensure that the final honey has a uniform texture, flavour and colour. In the process, the honey loses its character. Artisan honeys are very different. The honey is extruded in a way that preserves its fragrance, and will vary according to the flowers, season and year. Some will improve with age, developing a more full-bodied and mellow taste. Mono-floral (single-flower) honeys, in particular, have distinctive flavours, ranging from the intense caramel notes of heather honey to the lighter

citrus lavender honey. Local bee-keepers tend to have poly-floral honeys, simply because bees will forage for nectar in a two- to three-mile radius of their hives and this can encompass farmers' fields, local woods or parks and household gardens.

Honey tastes sweeter than sugar, although it has the same calorific value. The reason is that honey is made up of fructose and dextrose (glucose) rather than sucrose (sugar), and fructose tastes sweeter than sucrose. This perception allows you to add less honey than sugar to a dish, although care is needed in baking as sugar often plays an important role in creating the texture of the cake or biscuit. Honey also caramelises very quickly, so if using as a sticky glaze, add at the last minute.

All honey thickens with age, but the more fructose it contains, the longer it will stay liquid. Oilseed rape honey, for example, thickens very quickly as it contains a lot of glucose. If you need your honey to be liquid, set it over a low heat and it will soon melt. Similarly, if the honey has turned crystalline, heat it gently before cooking. Incidentally, if your honey becomes crystalline, it indicates that the honey has been extruded very simply. In theory, honey will keep indefinitely in a cool dark place, but occasionally it will ferment, if it has been exposed to water or dirt. A slight sound of fizzing on opening a jar is a warning sign of fermentation.

BUCKLAND ABBEY'S HONEY CAKE

The house will fill with the scent of honey as you bake this cake. It is from the National Trust's Buckland Abbey in Devon. They've reintroduced bees to the estate, continuing the monastic tradition of keeping hives in orchards, so depending on the time of year, the cake might be infused with lime or bramble blossom honey.

SERVES 10

115g/4oz honey
115g/4oz butter, softened
115g/4oz caster sugar
2 medium eggs

225g/8oz self-raising flour
1½ teaspoons mixed spice
about 100ml/3½ fl oz full-fat milk,
    as necessary

1 Preheat the oven to fan 170°C/gas 4. Lightly oil a 20cm/8in square or 18cm/7in baking tin. Line the base and sides with baking parchment and lightly oil.

2 If your honey is thick, gently warm over a low heat, then set aside until tepid but still runny.

3 In a large bowl, beat the butter and sugar until pale and fluffy. Gradually beat in the honey, followed by the eggs, a little at a time. Sift the flour and spice over the mixture and fold in, using a metal spoon. If necessary, add a little milk: the mixture should drop from the spoon in soft blobs. Spoon into the prepared tin.

4 Bake for 25–30 minutes (depending on the size of your cake tin) or until golden. Test by lightly pressing the cake with your fingertip; it will spring back if cooked. Transfer to a wire rack and leave to cool in the tin for 5 minutes. Turn out and leave until cold.

HONEY RUM BABA WITH PINEAPPLE

Don't be discouraged by the length of this recipe: it's easy to make and utterly delicious. Perfect for Christmas! It is easiest to make the dough in a food mixer or processor with a dough hook as it is a very wet, sticky dough. These rum babas are best eaten on the day of baking, but you'll need to soak the sultanas the night before they're needed.

SERVES 6

55g/2oz sultanas
185ml/6½ fl oz dark rum
1 teaspoon fast-action dried yeast
150g/5½ oz plain flour
pinch of salt
finely grated zest of 1 lemon
1 tablespoon honey
3 medium eggs, roughly beaten
55g/2oz butter, softened, plus extra for greasing

HONEY RUM SYRUP

185g/6½ oz honey
100ml/3½ fl oz water
finely pared zest and juice of 1 lemon
rum reserved from the sultanas

TO SERVE

1 medium pineapple, peeled, cored and diced
170g/6oz crème fraîche

1 Soak the sultanas in the rum overnight. The following day, drain the sultanas and reserve the rum. You'll need it for the syrup.

2 Put 1 tablespoon tepid water in a small bowl and sprinkle in the yeast. Mix thoroughly and leave for 10 minutes or until it has dissolved and looks frothy.

3 Sift the flour and salt into a large bowl. Mix the finely grated lemon zest into the flour. Tip into your food processor or mixer, fitted with a dough hook.

4 Melt 1 tablespoon of honey in a small saucepan over a very low heat. Pour into the flour. Beat the first egg into the yeasty water. Tip into the flour. Mix together with the dough hook. Add the softened butter and briefly beat until the dough looks smooth, then add the remaining eggs, one at a time, beating thoroughly until you have a glossy dough. Finally, beat in the drained sultanas.

5 Scrape the sticky dough into a bowl, cover with clingfilm, and leave in a warm, draught-free place for 2 hours or until doubled in size.

6 Liberally butter six 150ml/5fl oz dariole moulds. Since the dough is difficult to handle, dip your hands in some flour and firmly squash blobs of the mixture into the moulds. They should be about half full. Press the mixture down with a floured teaspoon. Cover with clingfilm and leave for 30 minutes or until the dough has risen to three-quarters fill the moulds. Preheat the oven to fan 190°C/gas 6.

7 Meanwhile, make the syrup by placing the honey with 100ml/3½ fl oz water in a small saucepan. Using a potato peeler, finely pare the zest from 1 lemon and add to the honey. Set over a medium heat. Stir occasionally until the honey has dissolved, then bring up to the boil and simmer for 5 minutes. Remove from the heat and add the juice of 1 lemon and the reserved rum. Strain into a jug.

8 Remove the clingfilm and place the moulds on a baking sheet. Bake for about 15 minutes or until golden brown; they should spring back when lightly pressed. Turn out on to a wire rack. While the babas are warm, pierce them all over with a fine skewer and dip each one into the syrup – making sure it is well soaked. Return each warm baba to its mould. Leave for 10 minutes then repeat the process. Leave in their moulds until cold. Strain the remaining syrup to remove any crumbs.

9 Prepare the pineapple: top and tail, then cut away its skin and remove the eyes. Quarter the pineapple lengthways and cut away the tough inner core. Discard the core and dice the flesh. Place in a bowl and toss in some of the honey rum syrup. Set aside until needed.

10 When you're ready to serve, turn out the rum babas, slice in half lengthways and arrange on individual serving plates. Drizzle each rum baba with extra syrup. Arrange some of the macerated pineapple on each plate, along with a spoonful of crème fraîche.

WALNUT BANANA BREAD

This is a lovely moist National Trust banana bread which keeps and freezes well. Try to use a locally produced artisan honey. The more flavour the honey has, the more aromatic your bread.

MAKES 10 SLICES

115g/4oz walnut halves, toasted and roughly
   chopped
115g/4oz butter, softened
170g/6oz good British honey

2 medium eggs, beaten
2 large or 4 small bananas, roughly chopped
225g/8oz self-raising flour
½ teaspoon mixed spice

1 Preheat the oven to fan 180°C/gas 5. Lightly oil a 900g/2lb loaf tin and line the base and ends with a long strip of baking parchment.

2 Place the walnut halves on a baking sheet and roast in the oven for about 5 minutes or until they start to release their fragrance. Leave to cool.

3 Put the butter, honey, eggs, bananas, flour and spice in a food processor and whiz until smooth. Add the walnuts and pulse until just combined. Pour the mixture into the prepared tin and level the top.

4 Bake for 30 minutes, then cover the top with foil to prevent it from browning too much, and bake for a further 30 minutes or until the bread is golden and well risen. A skewer inserted into the centre should come out clean. Leave in the tin for 10 minutes, and then turn out, remove the baking paper and leave on a wire rack to cool completely. Wrap in foil if not using immediately.

BIBLIOGRAPHY

Eliza Acton, *Modern Cookery for Private Families* (1855), Southover Press, 1993

Isabella Beeton, *Beeton's Book of Household Management* (1861), Chancellor Press, 1994

Anon, *Mrs Beeton's Every-day Cookery* (1909), Ward, Lock & Co., Ltd

Mary Berry, *Mary Berry's Baking Bible*, BBC Books, 2009

Natalia Borri, *Nikko Amandonico's La Pizza: The True Story from Naples*, Mitchell Beazley, 2001

Lizzie Boyd, *British Cookery*, Christopher Helm (Publishers) Ltd, 1988

Edward A. Bunyard, *The Anatomy of Dessert*, Chatto & Windus, 1933

Antonio Carluccio, *Complete Mushroom Book: The Quiet Hunt*, Quadrille, 2003

Robert Carrier, *The Robert Carrier Cookery Course*, WH Allen & Co., 1974

Sue Clifford and Angela King for Common Ground, *England in Particular*, Hodder & Stoughton, 2006

Linda Collister, *Bread: From Ciabatta to Rye*, Ryland Peters & Small, 2001

Margaret Costa, *Four Seasons Cookery Book*, Thomas Nelson & Sons Ltd, 1970

Alan Davidson, *The Oxford Companion to Food*, Oxford University Press, 1999

Sir Kenelm Digby, *The Closet of Sir Kenelm Digby* (1669), Prospect Books, 1997

Maria Elia, *The Modern Vegetarian*, Kyle Cathie Ltd, 2009

Jane Grigson, *English Food*, Penguin (1974), 1977

Jane Grigson, *The Observer Guide to British Cookery*, Michael Joseph, 1984

Dorothy Hartley, *Food in England* (1954), MacDonald & Co., 1964

Fergus Henderson and Justin Piers Gellatly, *Beyond Nose to Tail*, Bloomsbury, 2007

Jason Hill, *Wild Foods of Britain* (1939), Adam and Charles Black, 1941

Geraldene Holt, *Geraldene Holt's Cakes*, Prospect Books, 2011

Geraldene Holt, *The National Trust Book of Tuck Box Treats*, David & Charles, 1987

Good Housekeeping Complete Book of Preserving, Ebury Press, 1991

Miles Irving, *The Forager Handbook*, Ebury Press, 2009

B. James, *Wild Fruits, Berries, Nuts and Flowers: 101 Good Recipes for Using Them*, The Medici Society Ltd, 1942

Gerhard Jenne, *Decorating Cakes and Cookies*, Ryland Peters & Small, 1998

Sybil Kapoor, *Citrus and Spice: A Year of Flavour*, Simon & Schuster, 2008

Sybil Kapoor, *Modern British Food*, Penguin, 1995

Sybil Kapoor, *Simply British*, Penguin, 1998

Sybil Kapoor, *Taste: A New Way to Cook*, Mitchell Beazley, 2003

Nicholas and Giana Kurti (editors), *But the Crackling is Superb: An Anthology on Food and Drink by Fellows and Foreign Members of The Royal Society*, Adam Hilger, 1988

Richard Mabey, *Food for Free* (1972), Harper Collins, 1992

Mrs Marshall, *The Book of Ices* (1885), Smith Settle, 1998

Laura Mason with Catherine Brown, *Traditional Foods of Britain*, Prospect Books, 2004

Robert May, *The Accomplist Cook* (1685), Prospect Books, 1994

Harold McGee, *McGee on Food and Cooking*, Hodder & Stoughton, 2004

Mary Norwak, *English Puddings, Sweet and Savoury* (1981), Grub Street, 1996

Mary Norwak, *The Complete Book of Home Preserving*, Ward Lock Ltd, 1978

Sara Paston-Williams, *The National Trust Book of Christmas and Festive Day Recipes* (1981), Penguin, 1983

Sara Paston-Williams, *The Art of Dining*, The National Trust, 1993

Roger Phillips, *Wild Food*, Pan Books, 1983

Sir Hugh Plat, *Delightes for Ladies* (1609), Crosby Lockwood & Son Ltd, 1948

Elizabeth Raffald, *The Experienced English Housekeeper* (1769), Southover Press, 1997

F. A. Roach, *Cultivated Fruits of Britain*, Basil Blackwell, 1985

Claudia Roden, *A Book of Middle Eastern Food*, Penguin Books Ltd, 1968

Mrs Rundell, *Modern Domestic Cookery*, John Murray, 1853

Eliza Smith, *The Compleat Housewife* (1758), Studio Editions, 1994

Susan Spaull and Lucinda Bruce-Gardyne, *Leiths Techiniques Bible*, Bloomsbury, 2003

Constance Spry and Rosemary Hume, *The Constance Spry Cookery Book*, Weidenfeld & Nicolson, 1994

Richard Tames, *Feeding London: A Taste of History*, Historical Publications, 2003

Eric Treuille and Ursula Ferrigno, *Bread*, Dorling Kindersley, 1998

J. G. Vaughan and C. A. Geissler, *The New Oxford Book of Food Plants*, Oxford University Press, 1997

Robin Weir and Caroline Liddell with Peter Brears, *The National Trust Recipes from the Dairy*, The National Trust, 1998

Florence White, *Good Things in England* (1932), Jonathan Cape, 1951

Andrew Whitley, *Bread Matters: The State of Modern Bread and a Definitive Guide to Baking Your Own*, Fourth Estate, 2006

C. Anne Wilson, *Food and Drink in Britain* (1973), Constable, 1991

ACKNOWLEDGEMENTS

This book has come about through the hard work and support of many people. First and foremost, I would like to thank John Stachiewicz, Grant Berry and Brian Turner at the National Trust, whose enthusiastic support throughout the whole process has been invaluable. I would also like to thank everyone at Anova Books Ltd, in particular, my editor Cathy Gosling who has been patience itself, Kristy Richardson who has kept us all focused, Maggie Ramsay for her meticulous editorial work, and Alyson Silverwood for double checking everything. On the design side, thank you Nicky Collings for designing yet another beautiful book, and to Karen Thomas for her amazing photography and good humour; to Laura Urschel, her assistant, who kept our sugar levels down by making lovely salads, to Cynthia Inions for perfectly chosen props, and Bridget Sargeson and Jack Sargeson for their fantastic food styling. Food shoots shouldn't be such fun.

I would also like to thank Becca Spry, who first approached me about the book, and Geraldene Holt and Sara Paston-Williams for generously allowing me to use their recipes. My family have shaped my perception of British food, so a big thank you must go to my mother Helen Polhill. She will recognise some family recipes in this book. Last, but not least, I would like to thank my husband for his constant love and support.

PICTURE CREDITS

INDEX